The

PLAYSKOOL™

Guide for Expectant Fathers

The Best Information, Action Plans and Expert Advice for Your New Adventures in Daddyhood

Brian Lipps, M.D.

SOURCEBOOKS, INC.®
NAPERVILLE, ILLINOIS

Published by Sourcebooks, Inc.
P.O. Box 4410, Naperville, Illinois 60567-4410
(630) 961-3900
Fax: (630) 961-2168
www.sourcebooks.com

Library of Congress Cataloging-in-Publication Data

Lipps, Brian.
  Playskool guide for expectant fathers : the best information, action plans and expert advice for your new adventures in daddyhood.
    p. cm.
  Includes bibliographical references.
  ISBN-13: 978-1-4022-0934-5
  ISBN-10: 1-4022-0934-7
  1. Pregnancy–Popular works. 2. Fathers. I. Title.

RG525.L545 2007
618.2–dc22
                                        2007009098

Printed and bound in the United States of America.
BG 10 9 8 7 6 5 4 3 2 1

Contents

Part Three: Taking It One Month at a Time . . .143

Introduction

Congratulations—you have a baby on the way! If this is your first pregnancy, this is going to be one of the most exciting periods of your life. But it is likely to be one of the most challenging as well. If you are like most expectant fathers, you are probably feeling clueless about what is happening to your partner, you don't know what your role will be over the next nine months, and you don't know how to start preparing for what is going to be one of the biggest changes in your life. I know I felt that way when we were expecting our first.

When my wife was pregnant with our first son, it was a very exciting time for us. I was certainly proud and a little bit scared, but for the most part, I was completely oblivious to what was going on. Having a baby was a very abstract concept, and everything seemed to be centered around my wife. I wasn't exactly sure how I was supposed to be involved, other than "supporting her 100%."

Of course I had a certain amount of anxiety about their health and how the baby was going to change our lives, but mainly I felt like things were out of my control. So I did the only thing I could think of: I left everything to her and involved myself only when she asked. It wasn't that I didn't care, which I did a great deal; I was just unsure of what I should be doing. I figured this was "mommy time," and "daddy time" would start after the baby was born. As a result, I wasn't involved as much as I should have been.

When my wife was pregnant with my second son, I had the knowledge and experience from the first pregnancy to help me out. I wasn't so overwhelmed, and I naturally become more interested in what was going on and, not surprisingly, much more involved. By the time my third son was on the way, I definitely knew what to expect, I knew what my role was, and I knew what had to get done. As a result, I felt confident, in control, and fully engaged. By drawing on my experience, I even started making plans of action for each month of the pregnancy. This helped me to be even more proactive and involved.

I wrote this book not as another touchy-feely guide to emotional enlightenment and involvement but to show how any expectant father, given the right information and tools, can play a meaningful and supportive role in the pregnancy. It is my goal to help you understand and address the important issues that you will face over the next year, and to help keep you from feeling as clueless as I first did. However, I also realize that you are probably like most expectant fathers in that you don't have an intense desire to read everything there is about pregnancy, especially all at once. As a result, I tried to format this book in a way to be comprehensive but not overwhelming.

Sometimes information is presented in bite-size chunks, and other times it is outlined in great detail for follow-up referencing. The key is that you are exposed to the material repeatedly and in a way that helps you deal with an issue or solve a problem at the time it is relevant to you. Because the issues and problems you will be facing will not be coming all at once or necessarily in the same order, you will see a different type of format for the book. (And while your situation may be different, for ease of reading the expectant mother is referred to throughout the book as "mom" or "your partner".)

The first part of the book is intended to give you a quick overview of pregnancy and the birthing process, as well as issues arising when taking care of a new-born baby. It is intended to give you some "experience" with a typical and uncomplicated pregnancy so you are better able to put into context the details that you will be learning in the next two sections. You will probably want to come back and reread these chapters again after finishing the book to reinforce the material even more.

The second part of the book contains detailed information on issues that will be particularly important to you as an expectant father. I encourage you to initially skim it to get a feel for what's there, but I wouldn't spend too much time trying to learn it all at once. It will be more helpful to you as a detailed reference when you are actually in the process of addressing or dealing with a particular issue.

The third part of the book combines the timeline experience of the first part of the book with the detailed content of the second part. Each chapter explains what is going on with the baby, mother, and prenatal care during a particular month of the pregnancy. You will also be exposed to the feelings and fears that other expectant fathers experience during the pregnancy, and you will receive encouragement to assess your involvement in the pregnancy to make sure you are living up to your role as an expectant father. Finally, you will be given some suggestions for what you should be doing to stay involved in the pregnancy. Although it is not a comprehensive list, it should be a good starting point for you.

Good luck and best wishes on what will be one of the most exciting and life-altering experiences of your life.

Brian J. Lipps, MD

Part One

Understanding the Big Picture

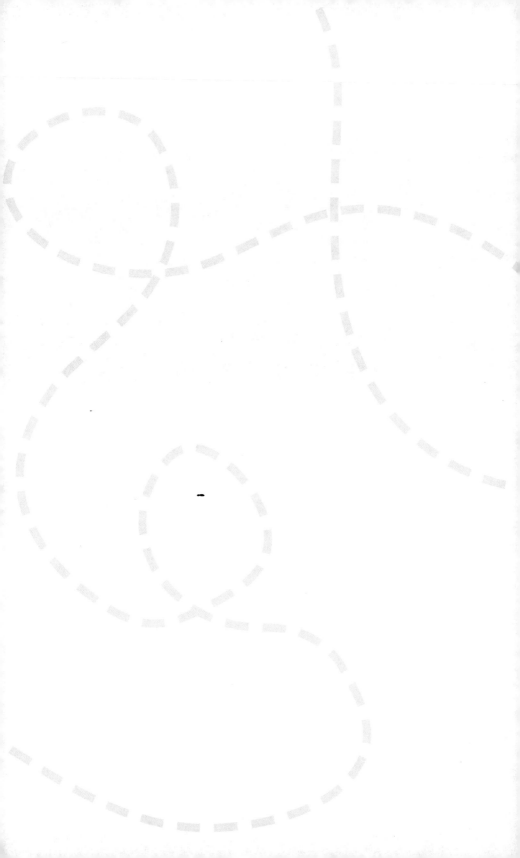

The Pregnancy

Many expectant fathers can go through an entire pregnancy without realizing what is actually going on with the mother and baby. Unless they are faced with an important decision to make, or are asked to do something, they usually leave most of the details to mom. The problem with this approach is that it is hard to follow what is happening with the pregnancy—and to deal with potential issues—if one is not aware of what's going on. Plus you are not being much help to mom, and you are missing out on one of life's great experiences. This is especially true because things can change very quickly from month to month. If you want to be more aware of what is happening and to be able to put everything in perspective, a good understanding of the pregnancy process and timeline is important.

The Importance of Genetics

Most people recognize that having a baby is a wonderful and miraculous event; however, not everyone realizes what a complicated process it is. Through a series of events, the genetic information of

In the long run, the diversity produced by genetic mixing is critical to humanity's ability to adapt and survive changes to our environment. In the short term, it means that our children are not destined to inherit all of our bad traits!

two people, in this case you and your partner, is combined to make a new mix of the two—your baby.

Although the process works well in the vast majority of cases, sometimes it doesn't, and it can lead to genetic diseases or birth defects. Realizing that something can go wrong often leads to anxiety and fear during a pregnancy. In order to better understand the risk, as well as what can be done to prevent or diagnose genetic problems or birth defects, it is important to have a basic understanding of genetics. This means knowing where our genetic information can be found and how we pass it on to our children.

Passing on Our Genes

All of our genetic information is contained in series of molecules called deoxyribonucleic acids, or DNA. Groupings of DNA that have a single purpose, such as the creation or control of something, are called genes. Each gene usually has two copies—one from the father and one from the mother.

It has been estimated that humans have between 20,000 and 100,000 functional genes, but nobody knows for sure. We haven't come close to figuring out what all of them do.

Genes are packaged into large structures called chromosomes. We inherit a set of 23 chromosomes from each of our parents, so we have a total of 46 chromosomes. Each chromosome in a pair looks similar, but on the level of the individual genes, they can differ significantly.

Two of our 46 chromosomes are called sex chromosomes because they determine what sex we are. Males have both an X chromosome and a Y chromosome (XY), whereas females have two X chromosomes (XX). Because women can only pass on an X chromosome, the baby's sex is determined by whether the man passes on his X or his Y chromosome.

When Your Baby Was Conceived

After your sperm met up with your partner's egg, something amazing happened. One of your sperm burrowed into the center of the egg and triggered a chemical reaction that made its outer shell become impenetrable to the other sperm. Your chromosomes were then released and combined with your partner's chromosomes. When this happened, your sperm fertilized her egg and it became an embryo. Over the next nine months, that embryo goes through a very complex but orderly process to become your baby.

The key to tracking your baby's progress during the pregnancy will be knowing the baby's gestational age and understanding the chronology of a normal pregnancy. There are three systems used to track a baby's progress during pregnancy: The first is based on weeks, the second is based on months, and the third is based on trimesters. All three systems are used extensively in books and on websites on prenatal care; this book will use trimesters here and months in Part Three.

> Of the millions of individual sperm that you initially released, probably only a few hundred actually make it far enough to fertilize your partner's egg.

The First Trimester

The first trimester of pregnancy started with the first day of mom's last menstrual period and will end after the third month, or week 13. It is a critical period of development when most of the baby's organs and structure are forming. The baby will be particularly susceptible to birth defects at this time. By the end of the first trimester, most of the baby's core structures will have formed and the baby looks human.

At first mom probably didn't realize that she was pregnant. A few weeks after the fertilization she may have begun to suspect, when she missed her period or was starting to have some unusual symptoms, such as nausea, fatigue, or going to the bathroom more often than usual. She probably confirmed her suspicions with a home pregnancy test.

It has been estimated that 15–30% of pregnancies end in spontaneous miscarriage during the first trimester. This can be thought of as nature's way of trying to make sure everything is developmentally okay before moving on.

Every month, the inner lining of her uterus enlarges in preparation for a fertilized egg. If one isn't available, this layer is shed approximately two weeks after ovulation—a process called *menstruation*. In order for the fertilized egg to be able to grow into a baby, menstruation has to stop. Hormones released by the fertilized egg, and then later the placenta, will stop her menstrual cycle and cause her to miss her period.

Although the baby is not very large during this first trimester (less than one ounce), the hormonal changes of pregnancy are going to have a profound effect on mom. In addition to the fatigue and morning sickness she might be feeling, she will likely experience frequent changes in her mood and emotions.

The Second Trimester

The second trimester will start in the fourth month, or week 14, and will end after the sixth month, or week 26. During this period the baby will be called a fetus and be recognizable as human. Most of the main body structures are going to be formed at this time, and the placenta will start providing nourishment to the baby. Although the sexual organs, spine, fingers, toes, and some other body parts will still be forming, the emphasis will be primarily on growth.

During this time the baby will start to collect a lot of fat under the skin, which will be important for keeping warm and providing energy later on. However, it will be awhile before the baby is pudgy! The baby will also start to suck its thumb, practice breathing and swallowing, and make urine. By the end of the second trimester, the baby's weight will have gone from just under one ounce to nearly two-and-a-half pounds!

Most mothers start to feel better at this stage because the physical symptoms of pregnancy have begun to improve. In fact, many women consider the second trimester to be the best part of pregnancy.

> Although many mothers will still experience a number of other unpleasant effects from the pregnancy during the second trimester, the effects are usually mild compared to those of the first and third trimesters.

Sometime past week 16, or the fourth month, the baby's movements are going to become more obvious. This will be a very exciting time for mom. By the fifth month (week 20), the baby's sex

Enjoy the second trimester of pregnancy. This is usually the best stage of the whole pregnancy, as mom feels like herself more than at any other time.

will be identifiable by ultrasound, and it will become obvious to others that mom is pregnant. Mom will also be starting to wear maternity clothes.

By the end of second trimester, or sixth month, your baby will likely be over 2 pounds, and mom will have gained 20 pounds—and there are still another three months to go!

The Third Trimester

The third trimester will start in the seventh month, or week 27, and end after the ninth month, or week 40. Although the baby could probably survive a premature birth at this point, the more time the baby has to grow and develop in the womb, the better.

Compared to the second trimester, the third will be more challenging for her, physically and emotionally. In addition to help with heavy lifting and chores, she will need a lot of comfort and emotional support. Better start practicing your back rub and leg massaging skills!

The rest of the pregnancy will be dedicated mainly to additional growth, storing of fat, and the final development of the brain and lungs. Although the lungs will be capable of breathing air by the beginning of the eighth month, they will really need more time to build up a chemical called surfactant, which helps to keep them from collapsing. Toward the end of the third trimester, the baby will be packed tightly in the womb and waiting to get out. In fact, after week 35, the baby could come at any time.

By this point mom will have gained a significant amount of weight, and her abdomen will be quite large, but the process is not over yet. She will probably be experiencing a number of distressing symptoms, including shortness of breath, heartburn, leg edema, muscle and back pain, difficulty sleeping, and fatigue. Her uterus will be so large that it will be continually pressing on her bladder, so she will have to go to the bathroom often.

Preparing for Birth

During the last couple of months of the pregnancy, mom's uterus will be changing in preparation for the big day. She will be experiencing some irregular uterine contractions, called Braxton-Hicks contractions.

For the baby to be able come out during labor, he will first have to get into position. This means rotating his body and getting his head to drop down into the pelvis. When this happens, the baby will be engaged. Although this is an important indicator that the baby is getting ready, it may still be weeks before labor actually starts. If the baby's head doesn't drop and engage by the time labor starts, the baby will be breech, and it may be necessary for mom to undergo a cesarean section.

In final preparation for labor, her cervix will start

It is not uncommon for first-time mothers to think that these contractions are the beginning of labor. Real labor contractions, however, are stronger, more frequent, and more painful. They will also not disappear when mom changes positions or walks around.

thinning out and opening up. This is critical because the cervix is blocking the exit to the birth canal.

2

Birth and Recovery

Many expectant fathers often feel anxious, helpless, and scared during labor and delivery. This is completely normal. By having a good overview of a normal labor and delivery, you will be amazed at how much you can follow what is going on. This knowledge and a strong sense of purpose in being there are the most powerful tools against the anxiety and fear that expectant fathers feel during this time.

Mom Is Going into Labor

A surefire way of knowing that labor is starting, or is going to start shortly, is when your mom's water breaks. This means that there is a break in the protective membrane that contains the amniotic fluid that surrounds the baby. When the membrane breaks, the amniotic fluid, or "water," rushes out. It can be quite dramatic, but that is not always the case. Sometimes it is more a leak than a gush, and the woman may not even be sure if the fluid is her "water" or a vaginal discharge. Sometimes it doesn't happen at all, despite being far along in labor, and it may even have to be broken by the doctor.

It can often be hard for the mother to know if the contractions she is feeling are still "warm-up" contractions or if they represent the start of labor. This is especially true if it is her first pregnancy. In fact, it is very common for nervous new mothers to go to the hospital thinking they are in labor, only to be told to go home. This is called false labor. If this happens to you, don't be embarrassed. It often happens, and you would be in good company.

The most commonly known part of labor is the strength of contractions. At some point the irregular and mild contractions that mom will be experiencing during the last couple of months of pregnancy will become more regular and pronounced. At first they will be between 5 and 20 minutes apart and last about 30–45 seconds. Eventually they will come 2–3 minutes apart and last about 60 seconds. By the time this happens, you will want to be in the labor-and-delivery suite. Therefore, when mom's water breaks or her contractions are increasing in frequency and intensity, it's time to call the doctor and go to the hospital or birthing center.

Checking into the Hospital

Television shows often depict labor as occurring suddenly, and you need to rush to the hospital before the baby comes. Although this can happen, it is very rare, and not common with a first baby. In fact, it is usually at least eight hours between the start of labor and when the baby is born.

Once you get to the hospital, you will need to check in and be admitted to the hospital's labor-and-delivery floor. For new fathers who are anxious and a little panicky, this process can seem incredibly slow and frustrating. Be prepared by having all of your medical insurance information available. This can help facilitate the process. It is even better if you plan ahead and preregister, which may let you bypass this step altogether.

After getting to your room, mom will be asked to change into a gown. A nurse will then place an elastic band or belt around her abdomen to monitor the contractions and the baby's well-being. This is called an electronic fetal monitor. The baby's heart rate will constantly be displayed and will usually be between 120 and 150 beats per minute. When the uterus contracts, you can see a spike on the monitor, as the baby's heart rate usually rises. The staff and the doctor will be using this information to help monitor the baby throughout labor and delivery.

The on-call nurse will then take a brief medical history to get a sense of mom's general health and discover if there were any problems during the pregnancy.

Controlling the Pain

If you and your partner have decided to have a traditional birth, one of the first things your partner is going to want—or perhaps even demand—is something for the pain. The pain is mostly caused by the contractions of the uterus from the opening of the cervix. Later, as the baby passes through the birth canal and causes stretching, there will be additional pain, which might be better described as great pressure. Fortunately, there are a number of different options for helping to lessen or control the pain.

The most popular form of pain control in pregnancy is the epidural. It involves placing a needle into the lower back and threading a tiny plastic catheter near the spinal cord. Medications can then be injected to dull sensations from the lower back. An important advantage to this is that the medications can go in slowly and be adjusted during the labor. However, because an epidural needs to be placed by an experienced anesthesiologist and requires careful monitoring throughout the labor, it is not available everywhere.

It's Time to Push

Assuming everything goes normally and mom's cervix is ready, she will be moved from her room to the delivery suite. Or, if her hospital room is set up to be a birthing suite as well, additional staff will be called in to set up the room for the delivery. You will know she is ready when the nurse or doctor performs an examination and then says that her cervix is thinned out, 100% effaced, and open, dilated 10 centimeters.

If mom is using the classic position for giving birth, she will be told to grab her legs, bend her head forward, and try to form a human "C." This is called the semi-sitting or semi-reclining position. Although it is very good for lining up the uterus and pelvis, it is not the only position.

Common pushing positions include:
- **semi-sitting or semi-reclining**
- **lateral or side lying**
- **kneeling or on hands and knees**
- **sitting or squatting**
- **dangling**

With the baby fully engaged, mom may have an overwhelming urge to have a bowel movement. This can be a very disturbing sensation and may keep her from wanting to push too hard. In fact, if she is pushing correctly, she may actually lose some stool. This is extremely common —a natural part of giving birth.

Initially, mom will likely be a little tentative and may not push as hard as she should. You should encourage her to really go all out. She should be doing three pushes per contraction, and each push should last about 10 seconds. Counting from 1 to 10 would be very helpful. It usually takes 30–90 minutes from the start of the pushing until the baby is born, but this can vary; it may be shorter if mom has had a baby before or longer if she is using an epidural or a lot of pain medications.

Baby Is Ready to Come Out

You will know that the baby is about to come out when somebody says that the baby has crowned. This means that the baby's head is starting to show. Sometimes when the baby's head comes out, it stretches the skin around the vagina to the point that it rips or tears it. To help prevent this from happening, many doctors will make a cut to help ease the stress. This procedure is called an episiotomy. It is not always necessary, so the doctor will decide at the time whether it might help or not.

After a couple more big pushes, the baby usually comes out fully. If you plan on catching the baby, keep in mind that it can be a bit messy and that he will be covered with a lot of bodily fluids and will be a little slippery. The key to making a good catch is being sure you are lined up and you are using two hands. The nurses or the doctor will show you how to do it best. Although you might be nervous about dropping the baby, if you are positioned properly and you are ready, it is extremely unlikely to happen. Also, the staff is usually waiting close to you—just in case!

Finishing up the Delivery

After the baby is born, he will still be attached to the placenta, which is still inside the uterus. To separate the baby, the umbilical cord has to be pinched (to prevent bleeding) and then cut. It is becoming customary for the father to be asked if he wants to do the honors. However, keep in mind that it is not uncommon for fathers to decline, and if you decide you are not comfortable doing it, that is okay.

Even though the baby is out, the uterus will still be undergoing contractions, albeit not as severe. These contractions help break away the placenta from the uterus. Once free, it may take one more push to get it all the way out. After the placenta has come out, it is time for the doctor to take a look at the cervix, vagina, and perineum for rips or tears. If something is found or there was an episiotomy, this is the time for sutures to be placed. If everything looks okay, the delivery will be technically over.

Recovering from the Delivery

As you might suspect, mom will need time to recover from giving birth to the baby. There are a number of issues that she is going to experience, and it might make her a bit grumpy. One of the biggest is the pain.

Many mothers might tell you that the pain after labor is mild compared to the pain of the labor. But you should realize that the pain is significant, and it will slow her down a bit after the birth, at least for the first few days.

Although the pain mom is going to feel after giving birth will be less intense than that of labor, it will still be bothersome. Depending on how traumatic the birth was, you can expect that mom will be sore for a couple of days in the area between her vagina and rectum. If she had an episiotomy or a tear, it may be a little longer. Generally, the pain will be gone within a week, and in the meantime, acetaminophen or ibuprofen should be enough to ease the pain.

Bleeding and Spotting

Having some bleeding or spotting after giving birth is normal and should not be a concern for you or mom. It is called lochia, and mom can take care of it using sanitary napkins. It may start out somewhat heavy and bright red, but it should get lighter in color over the first two weeks. If the bleeding remains heavy, does not go away, or has a foul odor, mom should discuss it with her doctor.

Bowel Movements

Many women don't have a bowel movement for a couple of days after the birth. If it is not causing a lot of abdominal or gas pain, or straining when going to the bathroom, it's probably not an issue. If mom is suffering from a bad case of hemorrhoids or had an episiotomy or a significant tear of her perineum, tough stools may be particularly painful. If this is the case, you might suggest that she talk to her doctor about stool softeners and local numbing creams.

Recovering from the Pregnancy

After nine months of pregnancy and dramatic changes to mom's body, it's going to take a little while for her to get back to normal. For example, many women develop swelling, called edema, during the last few weeks of pregnancy. Some expect that the swelling will go away immediately after giving birth, but, unfortunately, it can take a little while for all the fluid to be reabsorbed. If mom is anxious to speed up the process, she can talk to her doctor about water pills. Since her edema is likely to be gone after one or two weeks, you might try to discourage her from taking water pills. Although generally safe, water pills can cause dehydration and electrolyte problems.

Recovering from Cesarean Section

Sometimes a normal vaginal delivery isn't possible, and a cesarean section is necessary. If this happens with your partner, the recovery from the birth is significantly different. Because a cesarean section is major surgery, it understandably takes longer to recover. The average time spent in the hospital after a cesarean section is about 3–4 days (compared to 1–2 for a vaginal delivery).

In addition to staying in the hospital longer to make sure there are no postoperative complications, mom will experience a lot more pain. It will be very hard for her to hold the baby, get out of bed, or go to the bathroom for the first few days.

On the first day it is expected that mom will stay in bed and rest. There will be a lot of pain and it will be difficult to get up and go to the bathroom. Her intestines will likely still be stunned, so they won't be making stool. The doctor will probably leave the urinary catheter in place to make things easier. The doctor won't keep it in too long, though, because the longer it stays in, the higher the risk of infection. Her IV catheter will also stay in place to make sure she gets enough fluids and doesn't get dehydrated.

On the second day mom should be getting out of bed and moving around. The IV and urinary catheters should be coming out on this day. Moving around and changing positions is going to cause her a lot of pain, and she is going to need your help. Her appetite may or may not be coming back yet because the surgery combined with the pain medication can cause significant constipation and gas pain. The PCA pump should be stopped soon, and mom should be switched over to oral pain medications.

By the third or fourth day mom should be moving around without much assistance. As soon as she is able to take in and keep down liquids, her bowels are functioning (passing gas or stooling), and there are no infections or problems urinating, she will be able to go home. When she leaves, she will get a prescription for pain medications and stool softeners.

Sex

The doctor will request that your partner not have sex until after her six-week follow-up appointment. Giving birth can cause significant physical trauma, and it is not wise to rush. Since she is likely to be exhausted, experiencing hormonal shifts, and fearful of the pain, it probably would not be much of a consideration for her anyway.

The pain associated with a cesarean section is one of the most difficult things to deal with when recovering. To help with the pain, mom will likely be hooked up to a machine called a PCA pump, which will let her get pain medications when she wants. If the PCA pump isn't controlling mom's pain, she should let her doctor know.

Losing Pregnancy Weight

As you can imagine, losing one's pregnancy weight can be a very sensitive subject with many women. For some women, losing the weight can be done relatively quickly and without much effort. Others have a very hard time or may never lose the weight. On the average, it takes about 2–3 months to get back close to prepregnancy weight, but don't be surprised if it takes 6–12 months. Breastfeeding can help because a lot of fat, a major supplier of energy, is transferred to the baby. If the extra weight isn't melting away as fast she had hoped, you might make time to assess the type of food that you both are eating. It is not uncommon when there is a newborn in the house to rely on eating out, picking up fast food, or preparing quick, high-fat meals. You, dad, should make the effort to prepare healthy meals for her and you as well. Also, slowly easing in to an exercise routine is good for both general health and weight loss.

3

Newborn Care

Going through labor may seem like a long and challenging process, but it is nothing compared to the first six weeks after the baby is born. Although it might feel a bit overwhelming to think about what it takes to care for a newborn baby, it really isn't all that complicated. Initially, while mom and baby are still in the hospital, the doctors, nurses, and other hospital staff will share a lot of responsibility for taking care of the baby. When it's time to go home, however, it will be primarily up to you and your partner.

The First Few Minutes

Hearing your baby cry for the first time will be a dramatic moment. Not only does it drive home the reality that you are a father, but it also lets you know that the baby is okay. It signals that the baby is alive and breathing on his own. However, not every baby cries immediately after being born, and a short delay doesn't necessarily mean something is wrong.

Because babies start out breathing almost exclusively through their noses, it is important to suck out any fluids that might be in there and to make sure there are no birth defects. To do this, a suctioning device will be immediately placed in the baby's nose. If the baby hasn't started screaming yet, he will after this. Although most babies get through delivery fine, it is important to know immediately if there are complications. All newborns receive a formal assessment within the first few minutes of life. The results will be expressed as something called an APGAR score, and it will range from zero to ten. A score below a perfect ten does not mean that the baby is in trouble, but a score less than six usually means that the baby may need more intensive monitoring.

The APGAR Scoring System

The APGAR scoring system assesses the baby's skin color (Appearance), heart rate (Pulse), reflexes (Grimace), muscle tone (Activity), and breathing rate (Respiration). If the baby looks like he needs a little more attention than normal, he may get some help breathing or be sent to the neonatal intensive care unit (NICU).

If the baby is found to be doing well, the nurses will wipe off the fluids, put him under a heating lamp, and then bundle him up tight. This is very important because after being born, babies are susceptible to cold. It will also be important that he wear a little hat because a lot of heat can be lost through the baby's head.

The day your baby is born is a very special time for you, and you are likely to experience some very intense emotions. At first you are going to be very nervous about the baby's welfare. After finding out that he is okay, you are going to experience a lot of relief. Then when you finally hold him in your arms, you are going to feel overwhelming joy and pride.

Basic Medical Care

After you and mom have had a chance to meet your baby, the nurses will ask to take the baby to clean him more carefully and do some basic care. One of the first things they do is measure the baby's height and weight. This information is important because babies with low birth weights are known to have more problems and may need extra attention before and after leaving the hospital. A very large size for a baby may also indicate that something is wrong. On average, full-term newborns range from 6 to 8 pounds and from 18 to 22 inches. Preterm or overdue babies often fall outside this range.

After his height and weight are measured, your baby will have antibiotic ointment placed in his eyes to prevent any unrecognized infection that can lead to blindness. Even though mom was likely checked for potential infections as part of prenatal care, most hospitals require this for all newborns. Since babies can't really see very well in the beginning, a couple hours of goopy eyes is well worth the prevention of blindness.

Next up is a vitamin K shot, which is intended to help prevent bleeding, especially in the brain. Vitamin K is important for proper blood clotting, and because it doesn't pass through the placenta very well and a baby's liver doesn't make much of it, there is a risk of bleeding. Most hospitals give newborns an injection of vitamin K as a preventive measure. It isn't going to harm the baby, and it may prevent a serious problem.

> **If you or mom has any concerns about your baby being vaccinated, you should resolve the issue before the baby is born. Vaccinations (including the one against hepatitis B) are important and should not be withheld for fear of side effects.**

After that, your baby is probably going to get his first vaccination. Although most vaccines are given later in the pediatrician's office, it is becoming common to give the first of three hepatitis B vaccines while the baby is still in the hospital.

Hospital Monitoring

Whether the baby is spending time in the nursery or rooming with mom, he will be monitored by the pediatrician and hospital staff. While the baby is in the hospital, it is the hospital's responsibility to make sure he is doing well.

Temperature

It is important to monitor the baby's temperature to make sure that he doesn't get too cold or have a fever. Babies lose heat about four times as fast as an adult, and they don't tolerate being cold as well. On the other hand, fever during the first couple of days may represent an infection, which can be very serious. The temperature is usually checked once by rectum and then every four to eight hours under the armpit. Temperatures between 96.5°F and 98.5°F are considered normal.

Weight Loss

Whether newborns are breastfeeding or receiving formula, most lose weight over the first couple of days. They are losing fluids through their urine, stool, and sweat, and they are not taking in enough yet to make up for it. The staff will be watching to make sure that the baby doesn't lose more than 10% of his weight. Many mothers who are unsure of and anxious about breastfeeding can become very upset about the weight loss if they don't realize that it is normal.

Blood Tests

Before you leave the hospital, blood will be drawn from either the baby's heel or the umbilical cord and sent off to be tested for certain diseases. This happens for all newborns (states usually require it) so that any potentially devastating but treatable illness can be diagnosed and not missed. The results are not available immediately, and it is usually the responsibility of the state and the pediatrician to make sure that nothing is missed.

If this is mom's first time breastfeeding, it may be hard for her to know if the baby is latching on and getting milk correctly. If the hospital has a lactation specialist, you should definitely ask that she come by for a consultation as soon as possible after the birth.

Feeding the Baby

A big part of taking care of a newborn is making sure that the baby gets fed. It sounds obvious, but it isn't always easy. In addition to the anxiety from worrying that the baby is not getting enough, there is a lot of controversy about the difference between breast- and bottle feeding.

There may be a lot of pressure on a new mother to breastfeed her baby. It seems like it should be easy, but it isn't, especially if mom is breastfeeding for the first time. The baby may have a hard time latching on. Because you can't tell how much the baby is eating, mom might have a lot of anxiety about whether or not she is producing enough milk.

It is not uncommon for newborns to spit up after feeding. It can be distressing because a small amount of spit-up can seem like a lot. Despite the use of bibs, you may end up helping mom change the baby's outfit quite a few times a day. Make sure the baby burps after

Although there are many reasons to breastfeed a baby, it isn't necessary, and it may not be practical in some cases, such as with premature babies. The good thing about formula or bottle feeding is that you know how many ounces the baby is taking in, and you are able to help mom with this responsibility. On the other hand, if mom can consistently collect her breast milk in bottles using a breast pump, then you may be able to combine the benefits of breast feeding with the convenience of bottle feeding.

feeding, and try to keep him upright for 10–15 minutes afterward. Sometimes spitting up can be a sign of something more serious, such as gastrointestinal reflux or obstruction of the stomach. If the spitting up is relentless or severe, be sure to call your pediatrician.

Changing Diapers

Not only is changing diapers a necessary part of good childcare, it can also help you know if your baby is getting enough nutrition. As they say, what goes in must come out.

Not every baby urinates on the first day, but he should by the second. By the end of the first week, most babies wet their diapers between six and ten times a day. If your baby has not urinated within the first 48 hours, let your pediatrician know, for this can be a sign that something is wrong with his urinary tract system.

The baby's first stool is going to look weird because it is thick, sticky, and dark. This is called meconium and usually occurs within the first 24 hours. This is important to note because some babies are born with problems in their bowels, and a significant delay in stooling can be an early sign. Later on, the number of bowel movements and the characteristics of the stool will depend in part on whether he is breastfed or formula fed.

Keeping a close eye on the number of soiled diapers that your baby is making is an important way of monitoring the baby's food intake. This is especially true with breastfeeding, when you are unsure how much the baby is actually taking in. If for some reason the baby isn't getting enough breast milk or formula, you will see a decline in the number of wet diapers he is producing. On the other hand, if the baby is producing a lot of wet diapers, you can reassure mom that he is probably getting enough nutrition.

Babies that are breastfed tend to have more frequent, less smelly stools. This is because breast milk is more easily digested.

Another reason to be vigilant about helping mom change diapers is that if they are not changed frequently enough, the moisture can lead to irritation and yeast infections. Changing frequently, allowing the baby's bottom to air out, and using diaper rash creams can all be of help.

Make a chart and hang it on your refrigerator to track wet and poopy diapers. This gives you and mom an easy reminder of how the baby is doing throughout each day and can also be taken to your first appointment with the pediatrician.

Getting Baby to Sleep

Newborns spend a lot of their time sleeping, but they don't sleep for extended periods of time. Early on they also tend to have a reversed sleep pattern, spending much of the day asleep and tending to be more awake at night. At first this is nice because the baby can sleep quietly in his carrier while you go about your day. However, it will soon become apparent that the downside is you will often be up at night. Although it isn't always easy, mom should learn to match her sleep pattern to that of the baby and try to take daytime naps. If she doesn't, she is rapidly going to become sleep deprived. The same thing will apply to you if you are working during the day and not getting enough sleep at night.

> Don't underestimate the power of swaddling. Although it seems odd to bind them up so tightly, many babies need it to feel comforted enough to go to sleep. To them, it's like being back in the womb.

If the baby is having a hard time sleeping, consider darkening the room, lowering the noise level, and turning on rhythmic music. Sometimes swaddling the baby by wrapping his arms and legs tightly in a blanket can help him relax. Many babies are comforted by the limited mobility.

Figuring Out Why Baby Is Crying

Babies communicate through crying. It has been estimated that newborns cry an average of one to three hours a day, although it can sometimes seem longer! The most common reasons why a baby might cry are being hungry, being tired, and having a dirty diaper.

After making sure the baby doesn't have a soiled diaper that is irritating him, try to feed him. That usually does the trick. However, if the baby still appears to be hungry and not satisfied, take a look at his nose. If it looks stuffy, try cleaning it out.

If the problem wasn't a dirty diaper or stuffy nose, and offering food didn't help, it might be that the baby is overtired. Letting the baby "cry it out" for a little while to see if he will go to sleep may not be a bad idea. Keep in mind, however, that this might make you feel a little guilty.

Sometimes you and your partner may not be sure what the issue is. If the baby isn't hungry, uncomfortable, or tired, it could be that he is grumpy from being lonely or scared. Simply picking up the baby or using a pacifier may work. If the baby appears uncomfortable after being fed, consider trying to burp him. An overextended stomach can be very distressing. If nothing seems to work and something doesn't seem right, you or mom should call the pediatrician.

> **Discussing in advance such situations as the baby's crying can be very important. It gives you the opportunity to come to a consensus on dealing with common newborn-care problems when you are not sleep deprived and exhausted. It also gives you time to talk to your friends and relatives with children to see how they have handled similar problems.**

Keeping the Umbilical Stump Clean

The umbilical cord is a lifeline for the baby when he is in the womb. It has several blood vessels that need to be clamped off before being cut. Shortly afterward, blood clots will form and the clamp can come off, often just before the trip home. The remaining stump should periodically be cleaned, and eventually it will shrivel up and fall off.

It usually takes a couple of weeks before the stump falls off. Until then, it is a good idea to keep an eye on it and make sure it doesn't get infected. The staff at the hospital will clean the base and apply an antibiotic ointment around it. When you bring your baby home, it will be up to you to continue this treatment. Signs that it might be infected include redness, warmth, or something green or yellow oozing from it.

Getting Help

Taking care of a newborn during the first six weeks can be very difficult, especially if it is your first child. Nobody is born with the knowledge of how to take care of a baby. At times you and your partner are going to feel incompetent and get frustrated, but with a little bit of experience and practice, you will realize that you two can do it. The key is to recognize that it can be an overwhelming experience, and you should always be open to asking others for help.

Part Two

The Details

Diet, Health, and Safety

4

Pregnant women are intensely interested in diet, health, and safety issues. The importance of having a healthy baby and the fear of something going wrong generate a lot of strong opinions and emotions about these topics. Mom has no doubt already started reading about them. It is important for you to read about them as well, not only to help protect mom and baby but also to be able to inject a bit of calmness if mom becomes excessively anxious.

Diet and Nutrition

Good nutrition during pregnancy is essential because poor nutrition can be directly linked to birth defects and pregnancy complications. Also, the issue of weight gain and image can be a charged one. Eating well, taking proper vitamin supplements, and avoiding potentially dangerous food products greatly improve your chances of having a healthy baby.

Good Nutrition

Your baby undergoes rapid growth and development in the womb. In order for him or her to develop properly, mom has to take in an adequate amount of nutritious food. All too often, being pregnant, having food cravings, and "eating for two" are used as rationalizations for not eating the most nutritious meals. For example, although it is true that the baby needs fat to develop the brain and nervous system, it usually isn't necessary to add fat to the diet, unless mom has an extremely low body fat percentage.

Well-Balanced Diet

Eating properly during pregnancy means having well-balanced meals. Mom should be averaging an extra 300 calories a day during pregnancy. She should also be getting enough protein, fruits, and vegetables without adding extra fat and refined sugars to her diet. Calcium, folic acid, and other vitamins and minerals are also very important.

Vegetarian Diet

If mom is a vegetarian, she can continue to avoid meat during pregnancy without harming the baby. However, she needs to be more careful about getting enough protein and essential amino acids. If she doesn't eat animal products such as milk and cheese, she may have a problem getting enough calcium, iron, riboflavin, vitamin B_{12}, vitamin D, and zinc. Consulting a nutritionist would be a very good idea.

If mom is diabetic, her diet and glucose levels during the pregnancy need to be closely monitored by her doctor. Changes in medications and insulin can usually keep things under control.

Prenatal Vitamins

If mom's diet is well balanced, she should be getting an adequate amount of the important vitamins. However, because prenatal vitamins can offer many benefits without much risk, they are strongly recommended. The vitamins that doctors are particularly interested in supplementing are folic acid, calcium, and iron.

Folic Acid

Folic acid has been shown to reduce the incidence of birth defects of the brain and spinal cord. Although many foods are fortified with folic acid, there is no obvious downside to taking an additional 0.4 mg of folate per day.

Calcium

The average pregnant woman needs about 1200 mg of calcium every day to help the baby grow without affecting her bones in the process. Many women get much less than that. Because most prenatal vitamins contain only 200–300 mg of calcium, mom should eat calcium-rich foods such as milk, cheese, and yogurt, or she will probably need to take an additional calcium supplement.

Iron

Both the baby and the mother need extra iron to make enough red blood cells. A low level of red blood cells is called anemia. Most prenatal vitamins contain at least 30 mg of iron, which is usually enough to prevent anemia. However, it is not uncommon for a woman to be iron deficient at the start of a pregnancy due to previous menstrual bleeding, or to become anemic during the pregnancy. If she is or becomes anemic and has low iron levels, she will have to take a separate iron supplement. To help prevent this, she can eat food high in iron, including chicken, red meat, fish, and leafy green vegetables, along with enriched breads and cereals.

Vitamin C

Some people believe that vitamin C may help reduce the risk of a type of blood pressure disorder called preeclampsia. Whether that is accurate or not, getting a little extra vitamin C probably isn't going to hurt; extra or unused vitamin C is usually eliminated quickly by the kidneys.

Food Safety

Many people find it easier to focus on avoiding certain foods or food additives rather than concentrate on eating nutritious and appropriately sized meals. Mom is going to read or hear about certain foods that may be dangerous during pregnancy, and she will probably try to avoid them. In the examples that follow, however, the research data supporting the danger isn't as strong as many people make it out to be. Yet since it is safer to use a "why take a chance" approach, you and your partner should use your best judgment.

Caffeine

Many women forgo caffeine during pregnancy because it has been linked to birth defects, low birth weight, and miscarriage. Although this may be true, if mom can't totally give it up, she should limit her intake to two 8-ounce cups of coffee (300 mg of caffeine) per day. When doing so, she needs to keep in mind that espresso and cappuccino have a higher concentration of caffeine. Soft drinks and chocolate contain a lot of empty calories, but they have relatively little caffeine.

Artificial Sweeteners

Aspartame, also known as Equal® or NutraSweet®, is a special type of amino acid that is used as a food additive for low-calorie foods and drinks. To date, there is no evidence that it causes problems during pregnancy, but many doctors recommend avoiding it anyway. Saccharin should probably also be avoided. Sucralose, known by its trade name Splenda®, on the other hand, is not absorbed from the gut, so it is considered safe to use during pregnancy and breastfeeding.

Fish

Most types of fish are also safe to eat. Sushi or raw fish presents a small but real risk of parasitic infection and should probably be avoided. Certain fish, such as shark, swordfish, and mackerel, are known to have levels of mercury. There is some concern that mercury may cause developmental problems later in childhood.

Cheeses

Certain cheeses from unpasteurized or raw milk can place mom and baby at risk of infections from certain types of bacteria, particularly *Listeria*, *Salmonella*, and *E. coli*. Most doctors, but not all, agree that processed or pasteurized cheeses are safe.

Meat

Raw or undercooked beef or pork can place mom and baby at risk of bacterial and parasitic infections. To be safe, mom should eat meat cooked medium-well to well-done. Smoked meat can contain high levels of nitrates, but when consumed in moderation, it shouldn't be a problem.

Encourage mom to sit down with her obstetrician to go over what foods are safe during her pregnancy. Every doctor will have his or her own opinion, and it is always smart to follow the advice of your attending physician.

Liver

Vitamin A may cause birth defects if taken at high levels during early pregnancy. Because liver contains an extremely high concentration of vitamin A and isn't a critical part of a nutritious diet, it is prudent to avoid it during pregnancy.

Exercise

Exercising is a great way for mom to stay in shape and get through some of the discomforts of pregnancy. Exercising together is even better because it not only helps you to get into better shape, but it will also give you an opportunity to spend more time together. However, before starting a new exercise routine or continuing a previous one, mom needs to talk to her doctor to make sure it won't put her or the baby at risk.

Thinking about Exercise Options

When thinking about what types of exercise you might do together, keep in mind that her body will be radically changing over the next nine months. For example, certain types of exercise that require mom to support all of her weight (walking, running, hiking, dancing, or aerobics) might be okay early on but may not be as practical later in the pregnancy. Toward the end of the pregnancy, it may be better if you two participate in aerobic exercises that don't require her to support her whole weight, such as riding a stationary bike or swimming. In general, these types of exercises tends to be easier for her to perform and safer throughout the entire pregnancy.

> Although exercise is a good idea for most pregnant women, there are some conditions that may put her and the baby at risk. Her doctor may recommend avoiding certain routines if she is having twins or triplets, has experienced abnormal bleeding, is at risk for preterm labor, has high blood pressure, or has a problem with the cervix, placenta, or amniotic fluid.

A popular form of exercise is yoga. It is good for strengthening muscles, increasing stamina, and controlling breathing through relaxation. However, mom should make sure that she doesn't overstretch her muscles and ligaments, or put too much pressure on her abdomen. If she is interested in taking a yoga class, there are many available that are designed for pregnant women.

Staying Safe

Many women are used to following a vigorous workout routine before they get pregnant. Pregnancy, however, will cause many changes that can affect mom's ability to continue an aggressive routine. For example, hormonal changes and anemia can decrease her energy, her

Mom needs to stop exercising immediately if she becomes excessively short of breath, her heart rate is racing too fast (more than 140 beats per minute), she has severe pain, or she experiences any bleeding. If she is dizzy, becomes nauseous, grows excessively tired, or feels faint, then she has pushed it too far.

enlarged abdomen and breasts can throw off her center of gravity and balance, and she may be prone to episodes of low blood pressure. Lying on her back for too long, for example, may cause her enlarged uterus to block the large blood vessel in her abdomen from carrying blood back to her heart. To help keep both mother and baby safe, she should consider the following when planning her exercise program:

- She should limit herself to a moderate routine. Injury is more common with occasional attempts at extreme movements than with consistently moderate exercise.
- She should avoid overheating and getting dehydrated. Excessive heat and humidity can be fatal for pregnant women.
- She should avoid high-impact sports or other activities where she risks trauma to the baby. This includes such activities as biking, skiing, and horseback riding.

Tobacco, Alcohol, and Recreational Drugs

It can be hard for some pregnant women to give up smoking, alcohol, or recreational drugs during pregnancy. If this is the case with your partner, helping her to understand the risks is a critical first step in convincing her to try to give them up.

Tobacco

There is no question that smoking is dangerous to your unborn baby. It has been linked to miscarriage, preterm labor, low birth weights, and more. Whether it comes from mom or yourself, the carbon monoxide that tobacco produces can decrease the amount of oxygen your baby gets. If mom is the one smoking, nicotine can cross the placenta and lead to less blood getting to the baby.

Quitting smoking before or during pregnancy is a great idea, but it is certainly not easy. Using such nicotine products as gums, patches, or inhalers can help reduce the baby's exposure to carbon monoxide and other toxins, but it doesn't solve the nicotine problem. Although there are some antismoking medicines available, such as Wellbutrin® and Zyban®, they haven't been carefully studied to assess their risk of causing birth defects.

Alcohol

There is no doubt that heavy drinking, whether daily or during binges, is bad for the baby—especially during the first three months of pregnancy. Alcohol can lead to birth defects during this time, when the baby's organs are developing. Common birth defects from excessive alcohol consumption include abnormal facial features, heart and nervous system growth and development problems, mental retardation, and learning disabilities. It is not known how much alcohol is too much. It's unlikely that an occasional drink will hurt, especially after the first trimester.

Also, quite a few women have had one too many before they realized they were pregnant, and their babies have done fine. But the bottom line is, the less mom drinks, the safer she and the baby are.

> **For many women, abstaining from alcohol is not a problem, though for some it can be. To help mom avoid alcohol during pregnancy, you might consider cutting back yourself.**

Illicit drugs

People who use recreational or illicit drugs during pregnancy tend to have more complications than women who don't. It isn't always clear if the complications are caused by the drugs themselves or something else related to the mother, such as her general health or nutrition. What can be said for certain is that using recreational drugs is not in the best interest of the baby.

Marijuana

Marijuana is the most commonly used illicit drug during pregnancy. There may be some risk of preterm labor or low birth weight.

Cocaine

Cocaine can lead to severe high blood pressure, stroke, and even death in the mother. It can also lead to a number of complications during pregnancy, including preterm delivery, placental abruption, and low birth weight. Cocaine use has also been tied to sudden infant

> **When a pregnant woman takes a drug (legal or illegal), she should be aware of the health risks to the baby. Unless her doctor specifically says a certain drug is safe to take during pregnancy, she should assume that it is potentially dangerous.**

death syndrome (SIDS), neurological problems, and seizures later in the child's life.

Narcotics

Short-term use of prescription narcotics for pain relief isn't likely to hurt the baby. However, narcotic addiction places the baby at serious risk for complications during pregnancy and after birth. If mom is battling narcotic addition, she needs to tell her doctor and possibly be placed under the care of an obstetrician who specializes in high-risk pregnancies.

Medications and Supplements

Many women are nervous about taking any medication during pregnancy for fear of causing birth defects. This fear is often unjustified, but given the possible consequences, it is understandable. If mom was or is taking something that she thinks could be placing the baby at risk, she should call her doctor to make sure that it is safe to take.

Safety Ratings

Many drugs have not been specifically or extensively tested in pregnant women. To help alert doctors and other medical practitioners to the potential dangers of certain medications during pregnancy, the Food and Drug Administration (FDA) created a special categorical system.

Category A: Generally safe throughout pregnancy. (There are relatively few drugs in this category.)

Category B: Used frequently during pregnancy and appears to be safe. (Many over-the-counter medications fall into this category.)

Category C: More likely to cause problems for the mother or baby, but no clear risks have been identified.

Usually no formal safety studies are available to assess the risk, so it is not known for sure. (Most prescription medications fall into this category.)

Category D: There is a clear risk to the mother or baby, and these drugs should be used only if the benefits clearly outweigh the risks. (Most chemotherapy drugs to treat cancer fall into this category.)

Category X: Known to cause birth defects and should never be used during pregnancy.

Prescription Medications

It is often possible to check the safety rating for a medication on the Internet. If you find that mom is taking a prescription medication that falls in Category A or B, you can reassure her that they are very likely safe. If any of them fall into Category X, mom should stop right away and call her doctor.

Since pregnant women are often excluded from drug-testing trials, most prescription medications are Category C. If she is taking medications in Category C or D, she should not make any changes (starting, stopping, or changing dosages) on her own. You can reassure her that in most cases, short exposures to medications known to be associated with birth defects don't guarantee that they will occur. Depending on her

Medications that fall under each category include:

Category A:
folic acid, vitamin B_6

Category B:
acetaminophen, ibuprofen, insulin, prednisone

Category C:
Sudafed®, prochlorperazine (Compazine®), ciprofloxacin (Cipro®), fluconazole (Diflucan®)

Category D:
lithium, phenytoin (Dilantin®)

Category X:
isotretinoin (Accutane®), thalidomide, and diethylstilbestrol (DES)

medical condition, there may be a higher risk to her and the baby if she stops an important medication without consulting her doctor.

Over-the-Counter (OTC) Medications

Most, but not all, of the commonly used OTC medications, such as antacids, antihistamines, decongestants, laxatives, and antidiarrheals, are considered safe to use during pregnancy. However, it is always prudent to check the safety rating and to contact the doctor if there is any question. Among pain relievers, the safest is acetaminophen. Non-steroidal anti-inflammatory drugs (NSAIDs) such as ibuprofen are considered safe during the first two trimesters but not the third. There is a risk that NSAIDs can affect the closing of certain vessels in the heart. Also, it is generally advised that aspirin be avoided throughout pregnancy.

Herbs and Supplements

In the United States herbs and other supplements are not checked for safety. This means that there is no way to know if they are safe for the general population, let alone a pregnant woman. Just because something is natural does not mean that it is safe; for example, there are many poisons and cancer-causing compounds found in nature. If mom is taking any herbs or non-prenatal supplements, you might suggest that she stop taking them until she talks to her doctor.

General Safety

Many other questions about safety come up during pregnancy, and some of the more common issues are referred to below. You should discuss each of these with mom and develop a plan accordingly. As always, if you have any questions, be sure to have mom bring them up at her next doctor's visit.

Beauty Treatments

Many women use a variety of beauty treatments before and during pregnancy. Such treatments as facials, manicures, pedicures, and hair removal don't pose any danger to the baby, as long as good antiseptic techniques are used. The risk is unknown for other treatments that involve chemicals, including botulinum toxin (Botox), permanents, chemical peels, and wrinkle creams.

> It is important to discuss any big baby-proofing projects with mom prior to the birth. If any construction, additions, or painting will be done at your home, it's best to get it done prior to the baby's arrival.

Cats

Cats can carry a parasite called *Toxoplasma gondii*, which causes a disease called toxoplasmosis. They often get it from eating the raw meat of infected animals such as mice and birds. Exposure can cause a relatively mild illness in pregnant women that can lead to potentially severe birth defects in the baby. If mom has been exposed to toxoplasma previously and has developed immunity (it is estimated that 50% of Americans have), it's not an issue. Mom can get a blood test to check for immunity, but because the odds of something happening are between 1 in 1,000 and 1 in 10,000, it isn't often done. If you have an indoor cat, the best thing you can do to help prevent an infection is to take care of the cat litter yourself.

Cell Phones

With cell phones being so pervasive, staying in touch shouldn't be a problem. However, if you expect to be in an area where there is a hole in the coverage, it may not be a bad idea to have a backup system in place. Having a cell phone will also come in handy after the baby has arrived (when you need to make the all-important announcement calls!). Keep in mind that, while in the hospital, you will have to keep your phone turned off. This means you will be unavailable during the labor, and you will have to go outside to make any calls.

Family Bed

Many new mothers choose to have the baby sleep with them in bed. They feel that it is good for family bonding, and it makes breastfeeding more convenient. If mom plans on doing this, make sure that the mattress is firm. (This means no waterbeds.) You also need to make sure there isn't a lot of extra bedding or blankets. Having an extra foam mattress, such as those commonly used on changing tables, is a good way to make sure the baby has a firm surface to sleep on and makes it less likely that you or mom accidentally rolls onto the baby.

Hot Water

There is some evidence that women who have body temperatures consistently above 102°F during the first trimester may be at increased risk of miscarriages and birth defects. This doesn't mean that everyone who gets a cold and a fever is going to have problems, but it does mean that mom should avoid extended hot baths, hot tubs, whirlpools, steam rooms, and saunas. The occasional warm bath isn't likely to be a problem.

> Although a hot tub might help sooth some of mom's achy muscles, it may lead to an elevated body temperature. Given the uncertainty about the risk to the baby, she should avoid hot tubs during the pregnancy.

Infant CPR

It is extremely unlikely that you will ever need to use CPR on your baby; however, as the baby gets older and starts to move around more, there is the risk that he will put something in his mouth and choke or that he will fall into a pool or other body of shallow water. The reason that it is important to think about this now is that you'll have more time and motivation to learn it before the baby arrives. Also, if you repeat the course in a year, when the baby is starting to get mobile, you will remember more and be better trained. Infant CPR classes are widely available through the American Heart Association, the American Red Cross, and local hospitals. Classes are often available in the evening or on weekends to make it convenient for working parents.

Sex

Having sex during pregnancy is safe for most couples. If mom is at high risk for preterm labor, or has other complications, it may be better to abstain. Unless mom's doctor says otherwise, it is probably safe to have sex relatively late in pregnancy, as long as her membranes haven't ruptured and she isn't on her back for too long. If there is any question of danger to the baby, mom should check with her doctor first.

Studies show that sex during pregnancy is generally safe. Unless mom's doctor advises against it, there is no reason to avoid it.

Traveling

If the pregnancy is considered high risk, it is not a good idea for mom to be too far away from the doctor. Going to locations with inadequate health services or a high risk of infectious diseases is also not a good idea. Be sure to have mom check with her doctor before planning long trips or trips out of the country.

X-Rays

It is best to avoid tests that produce ionizing radiation, particularly in the first trimester. This means avoiding x-rays, CT scans, and angiograms, but not necessarily ultrasounds or MRIs. Mom might hear that ultrasound may not be safe, but there is no proof of this. It is important to realize that pregnant women can get seriously sick, and mom may need a radiology study using radiation. With proper shielding and limited doses, the benefits of radiation usually outweigh the risks. Before undergoing any such tests, be sure that mom consults with her doctor and lets the medical staff know that she is pregnant.

5

Prenatal Care

One of the most important parts of pregnancy is ensuring that both the mother and the baby get good prenatal care. Although women have been going through childbirth for ages without formal prenatal care, there is no denying its benefits. With proper prenatal care, many complications can be caught earlier, with better outcomes.

Selecting a Health Practitioner

One of the earliest and most important decisions in prenatal care is deciding who is going to be taking care of mom during the pregnancy and delivering the baby. For most women, the health practitioner is a medical doctor who specializes in pregnancy. However, if there is nothing in mom's medical history indicating that she is at high risk for complications, she can choose to have her baby delivered by her family doctor or a licensed midwife.

Obstetrician

Obstetricians are the most trained and experienced practitioners for both normal and abnormal pregnancies. Although most pregnancies are uncomplicated, problems can arise, and the mother and baby could be at risk of injury or even death. Obstetricians are trained to identify high-risk situations and to act if the mother or baby is in distress. A potential downside is that an obstetrician may be too conservative or unsupportive of how mom would like to do things. There might also be concerns that obstetricians are impatient and too quick to give up on spontaneous vaginal birth, or may overuse medications or cesarean sections.

> **Until the twentieth century, childbirth was considered very dangerous, and many women and babies died in childbirth.**

Family Physician

Many family physicians (general practitioners) have the training and experience to offer prenatal care and to deliver babies. However, most family physicians are not trained to take care of high-risk pregnancies. Your family doctor will likely refer mom to an obstetrician who specializes in high-risk pregnancies if mom has any of the following:

- A chronic medical condition such as diabetes, high blood pressure, lupus, or epilepsy
- A disorder of the heart, kidney, liver, or blood
- Previous miscarriages, premature deliveries, stillbirths, or babies with birth defects
- A history of multiple babies (including twins)

Licensed Midwife

Many people feel that obstetricians and family doctors are too "medical" and don't share their holistic approach to childbirth. There is some truth to that. As a result, many women feel more comfortable using midwives, who are specially trained and licensed to deliver babies, often accompanied by a physician. For most routine and uncomplicated pregnancies and births, a licensed midwife is an acceptable alternative, especially if you are in the hospital. However, if mom develops factors for a high-risk pregnancy or the baby is being delivered outside of a hospital, you need to evaluate the situation very carefully. Being under the supervision of a physician who isn't present during prenatal care or at the delivery is not the same as being under the direct care of a doctor. Although complications occur rarely, when they do, a physician's presence can prevent a serious, possibly deadly outcome.

Medical History

During the first prenatal visit, the doctor will conduct an extensive review of mom's medical history. Although potentially tedious and time-consuming, a review of this information is very important in helping the doctor to take care of mom and to assess if there is a higher-than-normal risk for complications during the pregnancy.

Gynecological History

Most women of childbearing age have a relatively short medical history. As a result, the history review is focused primarily on a woman's gynecological and obstetrical history.

Menstruation

Even though mom isn't menstruating now that she's pregnant, it is important to know about her cycle to assess the accuracy of the due date. The type of birth control your partner used, or if she underwent in vitro fertilization (IVF), would also be important information. The latter is particularly important because of its association with multiple births.

Sexual History

It is important that the doctor obtain an accurate and truthful recounting of your partner's sexual history. It is of particular importance if she previously had any sexually transmitted diseases. Complications from previous infections can increase the risk of the pregnancy occurring outside the womb or being an ectopic pregnancy.

Abortions

In most cases, previous abortions will not affect mom's current pregnancy. However, there is some concern that multiple second-trimester abortions may be associated with premature births.

Fibroids

Having fibroids won't affect a pregnancy in most instances; however, if they are particularly numerous or large, or if there was major surgery on the uterus to remove them, it could be a problem. Fibroids can sometimes lead to an increased risk of ectopic pregnancy, miscarriage, placental problems, and labor complications.

Previous Surgeries

Surgeries involving the uterus (e.g., cesarean sections or removal of large fibroids) can increase the risk of the uterus rupturing during labor. Depending on her surgical history, it is possible that mom may be required to undergo a cesarean section.

Obstetrical History

If mom has had previous pregnancies supervised by another doctor, and the medical records are not available, she should try to recount as much detail about them as she can. In general, a woman's first pregnancy is a good indicator of how future pregnancies will likely go.

Hyperemesis Gravidarum

If mom experienced hyperemesis gravidarum (a severe form of morning sickness) in a previous pregnancy, there is a good chance that she is going to have problems this time around.

Ectopic Pregnancy

A previous ectopic pregnancy, or one that occurred outside the womb, increases the risk of having another. Although relatively rare, they are more common if there has been pelvic inflammatory disease, previous surgery with scarring, or intrauterine device (IUD) use.

Pregnancy Loss

Spontaneous miscarriages during the first trimester of pregnancy are relatively common. In fact, many women mistake them for a particularly heavy period and may not have even known that they were pregnant. However, the loss of the baby later in the pregnancy is of more concern to the physician. It may be due to a problem with the cervix or placenta, or another medical condition that is treatable if recognized early enough.

> In a perfect world, your medical records would be available to all your doctors, anywhere in the world and at any time. However, until there is a universal electronic medical record system, it is important to encourage mom to keep a log during this pregnancy for reference in future pregnancies.

Premature Labor

There are several risk factors for premature labor, and many are identifiable by the doctor. These include infections, incompetent cervix, and placenta previa, to name a few. If mom experienced premature labor before, it should be noted and lead to a more thorough assessment by the doctor.

Labor Complications

If mom had any life-threatening complications during a previous labor, it is obviously important that her doctor be aware of that. However, there are a number of other potential complications that she may not have realized were out of the ordinary. For example, did her labor stall and require the use of medications to help it along? Did the baby have problems requiring the doctor to use forceps or a vacuum extractor?

Birth Defects

If any of mom's previous pregnancies involved birth defects or genetic disorders, the doctor will need to know. Depending on the defect and the family history, genetic counseling and testing may be necessary.

General Medical History

An increasing number of women with chronic illnesses, such as high blood pressure and diabetes, are getting pregnant. Because of the risk a chronic illness may pose to both the mother and the baby, it is important that mom's doctor be aware of any she may have.

Asthma

Asthma can complicate a pregnancy, particularly if mom has frequent or severe attacks. During an attack, oxygen levels may decrease, thus putting the baby at risk. Since most asthma medications are safe during pregnancy, it is important not to undermedicate.

Cancer

Fortunately, cancer occurring during pregnancy is very rare. However, most treatments for cancer, including chemotherapy and radiation, are potentially harmful to the baby. Even if mom has had cancer in the past and is in remission, it is important that she make the appropriate medical records available to her doctor.

Diabetes

Uncontrolled diabetes during pregnancy can increase the risk of miscarriage, birth defects, and complications during labor. Excellent control of diabetes through frequent blood checking and proper use of insulin is important.

Heart Disease

Being pregnant places a tremendous strain on the body, especially the heart. In fact, during pregnancy, the heart has to work about 50% harder. If mom was ever diagnosed with a heart murmur, had something wrong with her heart valves, or experienced any other heart problem, she needs to make sure her doctor has access to the appropriate medical records.

High Blood Pressure

High blood pressure can complicate a pregnancy, particularly if the hypertension is not well controlled. There is a higher risk of preeclampsia, placenta abruption, and poor fetal growth. Close monitoring and frequent testing of the baby's health will be necessary.

Seizure Disorders

Almost all medications used to treat seizure disorders are associated with a higher risk of birth defects. Discontinuing seizure medications is often difficult, if not impossible, and may pose more of a risk than maintaining the medications. Close monitoring for birth defects with ultrasound exams is important, as is additional monitoring from mom's neurologist.

Urinary Tract Problems

The most common urinary problems are bladder or urinary tract infections (UTIs) and kidney stones. If mom suffers from frequent

UTIs, there is a higher risk that she will develop pyelonephritis, an infection of the kidney, which can increase the risk of a premature delivery.

Family History

Many birth defects, genetic diseases, and other conditions affecting pregnancy tend to run in families. Before mom meets with her doctor, you both should ask family members about complicated pregnancies they might have had, or about any diseases that they think may be genetic. Disorders involving numerous or close relatives, particularly parents and siblings, are more relevant than rare instances or those involving a distant relative.

Mom's job may involve exposure to certain chemicals or radiation that may pose a risk to the baby. By talking to the doctor about her job, she will get a better idea of what the potential dangers are and whether she needs to talk to her employer about restricting certain work activities while she is pregnant.

Social History

This is the part of the initial examination where the doctor learns about your partner's use of tobacco, alcohol, and/or recreational drugs. Although it would be easy for your partner to downplay her experiences with them, it is important for both her and the baby that she be honest.

Vaccination History

Mom's doctor will want to know what vaccines she has and has not received. This is important because certain illnesses caused by viruses can cause birth defects if they occur during pregnancy. Also, certain vaccines probably should not be given during pregnancy. Since most people receive their vaccinations as children, it is helpful to obtain the records from her pediatrician, if at all possible.

Medication History

Some medications are not safe during pregnancy and may cause birth defects. During the first visit, mom's doctor will review all of her medications, including over-the-counter drugs. The doctor will also want a complete history of supplements she's taking, including herbal supplements. Mom should either bring all of her medication bottles with her or have a complete list of them. Any medications she stopped but was taking either shortly before or while pregnant should be noted as well.

Initial Testing

During the initial visit to the doctor, mom will undergo a battery of blood, urine, and other prenatal tests. Most of these tests are standard for every pregnant woman, because it is important to know if something exists that may place the baby or the mother at risk.

Checking Blood Counts

Many women of childbearing age are anemic because of blood loss during menstruation. Changes in pregnancy can cause the anemia to get worse, so a complete blood count (CBC) and iron studies are ordered at the beginning of the pregnancy. The blood count will be checked periodically throughout the pregnancy, usually around the fourth month, and again after the birth.

White Blood Count (WBC): White blood cells help fight off infection. If mom develops a fever, the doctor will check for a high WBC as a sign of infection.

Hematocrit (Hct): Hematocrit is the fraction of blood that is made up of red blood cells. A low Hct indicates anemia.

Hemoglobin (Hb): The most important part of the red blood cells is hemoglobin. Many doctors use hemoglobin instead of hematocrit to monitor for anemia.

Platelets (Plts): Platelets help the body to stop bleeding. The doctor will check in the beginning to make sure there isn't a problem with the platelets, which may lead to a problem during labor.

Iron Studies: Iron is necessary for the body to make hemoglobin and thus red blood cells. Many women are iron deficient because of menstruation. During pregnancy, the baby will have a high demand for iron, which can lead to a worsening of iron deficiency during pregnancy.

Determining Blood Type

Because there are different blood types (A, B, AB, O), it is important to know your partner's, in case there is excessive bleeding and a blood transfusion is needed. There is another red blood cell marker, called the Rh marker, that is also very important to know during pregnancy. If mom has blood that is Rh-negative, for example, and she was exposed to Rh-positive blood during a pregnancy, she could have developed antibodies against the Rh factor. This can lead to severe anemia if your baby has Rh-positive blood. With early recognition and administering of special antibodies, it is possible to keep the mother from developing these antibodies.

Screening for Infections

The doctor will be screening for bacterial and viral infections. You or mom should not be insulted that her doctor wants to check for sexually transmitted diseases at this time, because many of the tests are required by law. Society has a duty to your unborn child, and effective treatment is available to protect the baby.

Chlamydia

Chlamydia is the most common infection passed from mother to baby. It is often without symptoms and may lead to pneumonia or eye infections. Testing involves taking a culture of the cervix during a pelvic exam. Treatment with antibiotics will cure it but not prevent its reoccurrence.

Gonorrhea

As a systemic infection, gonorrhea is known to cause a serious eye infection (conjunctivitis) and blindness. Testing involves taking a culture of the cervix during a pelvic exam. Treatment with antibiotics will cure it but not prevent its reoccurrence.

Syphilis

Unrecognized syphilis infection can lead to serious birth defects, including nervous system damage and stillbirth. Testing for signs of it in the blood and treatment with antibiotics are routine and critical. The key is to eradicate it before the fourth month.

Hepatitis B

Having an unrecognized hepatitis B infection, or being a carrier (having the virus but not the disease), places the baby at risk at birth. Until then, the baby is protected. Testing involves taking a blood sample and looking for certain proteins (antigens) that are produced by the virus. If they are present, extra care will be taken to ensure that contact between the baby and the mother's blood at the time of birth is limited. Also, with advance knowledge, administration of a special immunoglobulin and the vaccine can be arranged, which will make the risk of transmission very low.

HIV

There is a high risk of transmission of HIV from the mother to the baby, if the virus is untreated. It has been found that aggressive treatment of the virus during the pregnancy can reduce the chances of it being passed on to the baby. As a result, screening for HIV is becoming routine, regardless of risk factors. Testing involves taking a blood sample and looking for antibodies against the virus (these antibodies don't protect the carrier, however). If detected, they are confirmed with another, more specific test.

Testing for Immunity

The doctor also needs to know if mom has immunity and antibodies against such viruses as German measles (rubella) and chicken pox (varicella). Both of these diseases can cause serious harm to your baby if they occur during pregnancy.

> **Most women have antibodies against the rubella virus because they have had the vaccine. Most women have antibodies against the varicella virus because they have had the illness or the vaccine.**

Getting a Pap Smear

Cervical cancer and other disorders of the cervix can have serious effects on the pregnancy. If a Pap smear hasn't been recently performed, mom will get one as part of her physical examination.

Checking the Urine

Mom's urine will be checked every visit for signs of diabetes, certain types of kidney disease, and urinary tract infections. All three are associated with pregnancy. The urine is usually checked with a dipstick, but it may be sent out to a lab for further testing.

Checking for Diabetes

With diabetes, there isn't enough insulin to keep blood glucose levels under control. When the glucose level is too high, it spills over into the urine and can be detected using a urine dipstick. The urine is checked every visit; if it is high and mom doesn't have a history of diabetes, she will be checked for a type of diabetes that occurs during pregnancy, commonly called gestational diabetes (which will be discussed later).

Checking for Infections

There is a higher risk of developing kidney infections during pregnancy. It is thought to be due in part to pregnancy hormones making the tubes connecting the kidneys to the bladder (ureters) less able to keep urine infected with a bladder infection from backing up into the kidneys.

So, in addition to testing for signs of inflammation with a urine dipstick (white blood cells, red blood cells, and some protein), urine is often sent to the lab to see if there are bacteria growing in it. If bacteria are found, the infection will be treated with antibiotics.

Ultrasound

Ultrasound has radically changed prenatal care. Before it came along, there was no easy way see what was going on inside of the uterus. Unlike other radiology procedures, where x-rays or other radiation is involved, ultrasound poses no risk to the baby.

Although ultrasound is very good, it is not perfect. It cannot detect every birth defect, and sometimes there can be a false positive result (where something appears wrong but it is really not). New 3D ultrasounds are making it easier to assess birth defects, but they are not widely available.

First Ultrasound

The baby's due date is usually determined by when mom's last menstrual period ended. Because of the possibility of irregular menstrual cycles as well as confusion about when it actually ended, it is not uncommon for the estimated due date to be wrong. Around week 6, your doctor will use ultrasound to take measurements of the baby and compare the results with what is expected at that date. If there is a serious discrepancy, the doctor will usually consider the ultrasound more accurate and make the appropriate change in the estimated delivery date.

Second Ultrasound

Usually by week 20, it is possible to determine the sex of the baby and screen for obvious birth defects and deformities. The sex of the baby is initially determined mainly by whether a penis or scrotum can be seen. If the baby cooperates and provides a good look, you can be pretty sure what the sex is. Occasionally, there may be some ambiguity, but this is relatively rare.

Screening for Birth Defects

After the first semester, when most of the organ development is complete, usually between weeks 15 and 18, mom will undergo screening for certain birth defects, particularly Down's syndrome and neural tube defects. Because these tests are notorious for false positives, they can be a great source of anxiety, especially if they result in an amniocentesis (discussed below).

Maternal Serum Alpha-Fetoprotein (MSAFP)

Abnormally low levels of MSAFP can be used as a screening tool for Down's syndrome. However, it is not very sensitive by itself and catches only about 1 in 4 cases. A high level of MSAFP can indicate a possible neural tube defect such as spina bifida, spinal column deformity, or anencephaly (the absence of part or all of the brain).

Human Chorionic Gonadotropin (hCG)

High levels of hCG have been associated with Down's syndrome. When combined with low levels of MSAFP, the results are more sensitive for Down's syndrome.

Estriol

Low levels of estriol, a type of estrogen, combined with abnormal MSAFP and hCG increases the sensitivity for Down's syndrome. Measuring of MSAFP, hCG, and estriol is called the "triple screen test."

Amniocentesis

The most common purpose for an amniocentesis is to look for Down's syndrome, which is caused by having three copies of chromosome 21. However, it can also test for at least 40 other problems, including neural tube defects, cystic fibrosis, Tay-Sachs disease, hemophilia, and sickle cell disease. An amniocentesis can also be used to assess the maturity of the baby's lungs, if there are considerations of inducing labor earlier than normal.

> The triple screen test has improved the ability of doctors to accurately screen for Down's syndrome, but there are still a significant number of false positives. A positive result needs to be followed up with an amniocentesis before the diagnosis is made.

Amniocentesis involves locating the baby and placenta with ultrasound and placing a long, hollow needle through the abdominal wall and uterus and into the amniotic sac. A small amount of fluid is then removed and analyzed. Because amniocentesis is an invasive procedure, there are risks. Using ultrasound and waiting until there is enough amniotic fluid (weeks 15–20) has reduced the risks. The most common complications are cramping, spotting, and amniotic fluid leakage. However, there are risks of infection, bleeding, and trauma to the baby, placenta, and umbilical cord. Worst-case scenarios include premature labor, miscarriage, or loss of the baby.

> An amniocentesis is used to test for the following:
> - Down's syndrome
> - Other chromosomal abnormalities
> - Genes causing certain diseases
> - Neural tube defects
> - Rh incompatibility
> - Baby's lung immaturity

Glucose Tolerance Testing and Gestational Diabetes

Gestational diabetes is one of the most common complications of pregnancy. It occurs in women who can't make enough insulin to keep blood glucose levels normal due to the increased weight from a pregnancy.

During the seventh month, mom will undergo a glucose tolerance test to see if she might have gestational diabetes. This could happen sooner if she is at high risk or her urine test was abnormal. Screening involves mom drinking a less-than-pleasant glucose drink and waiting an hour. Her blood is then taken to measure the blood glucose level. If the blood glucose level is high, it may mean that mom is at risk for gestational diabetes. Because there is a risk of a false positive result, a positive result will be followed by a more comprehensive test.

A positive one-hour screening test is usually followed by a three-hour diagnostic test. If mom has to undergo it, she will be asked to fast overnight before the test. Her blood level will be checked first, and then she will be asked to drink a different glucose solution. Three additional blood samples will be taken every hour over the next three hours. If two of the four blood levels are high, the test is considered positive, and gestational diabetes will be diagnosed.

Baby Well-being Tests

Toward the end of the pregnancy, the doctor may perform one or more tests to assess the baby's well-being. These are usually done only during a high-risk pregnancy, and in most cases, everything turns out fine. However, depending on the results, mom may be watched more closely than normal.

Nonstress Test

A nonstress test involves measuring the baby's heart rate in response to its movements. During the test, every time mom feels the baby move, she will press a button. After 20 minutes or more, the doctor will look for episodes of the baby's increased heart rate, called accelerations. If enough accelerations are present, the test is "reactive," and the baby is probably doing fine. If there aren't enough accelerations, the test is "nonreactive." In most cases, the baby still is doing fine, but closer monitoring is required.

Contraction Stress Test

The contraction stress test is similar to the nonstress test, but the changes in the baby's heart rate are timed with contractions of the uterus. It is used when the nonstress test is inconclusive, or the doctor wants further proof that everything is fine. It requires at least three good contractions within a 10-minute period to be interpreted properly. Contractions may have to be induced (by medication or nipple stimulation). Women at risk of premature labor or placenta previa should not get this test. Unlike the nonstress test, the doctor is looking for slowing of the heart (decelerations) after a contraction. If none are present, the test is "negative," and all is likely well. If decelerations are present (or something doesn't look totally normal), additional investigation is required.

Biophysical Profile

The biophysical profile involves careful inspection of the baby with an ultrasound and monitoring of the baby's heart rate, similar to a nonstress test. The baby will be assessed for body movements, body tone, breathing movements, amount of amniotic fluid, and heartbeat accelerations. Two points are given for a normal result in each of these areas. A score of 8 or more suggests that everything is fine. A score of 6 suggests that things are probably fine, but follow-up testing would be prudent. A score of less than 6 indicates further evaluation is necessary.

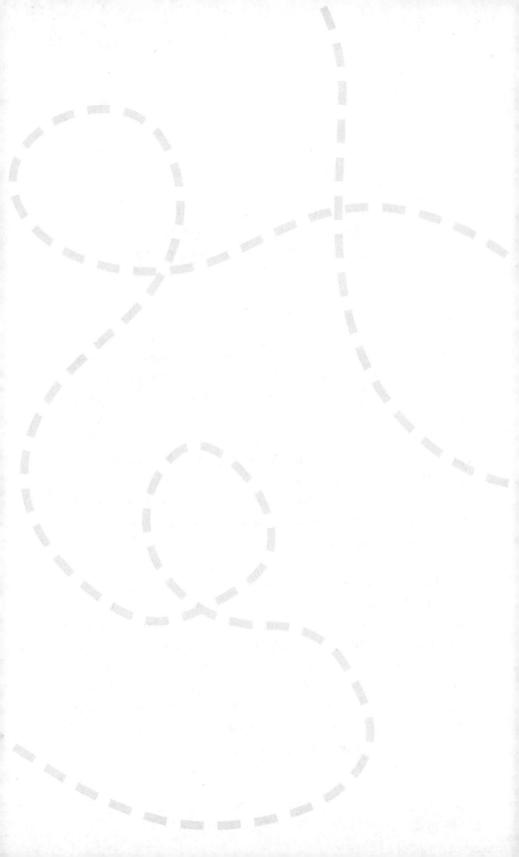

6

Planning Your Baby's Birth

For many women, undergoing childbirth is one of the most important and special times of their lives. They want the experience to be absolutely perfect, so they will spend a lot of time deciding exactly what they want out of the birthing process and plan it accordingly. Although an expectant father often has a say in what might happen, the mother is usually far more knowledgeable about the process and has much stronger opinions. Nonetheless, it is important for you to be extensively involved in the process, because it is extremely common for things not to turn out quite as expected. The more you know about what mom considers important when she is planning the birth, the easier it will be for you to help her when the time comes if things go differently.

Deciding Where the Baby Is Going to Be Born

Deciding where the baby is going to be born often, but not always, goes hand-in-hand with the choice of practitioner. Different practitioners have their own preference and comfort level concerning where they will help deliver the baby.

Hospital

Most people have their babies in the hospital under the care of an obstetrician. This is the safest way to go because of the resources available in case something goes wrong. However, it comes at the cost of decreased control and a more clinical environment. Some women may be concerned that having a baby in the hospital might increase their chance of having an unnecessary cesarean section.

Home Births

Before the twentieth century, most births in the United States occurred at home. With adequate preparation, giving birth at home with a certified midwife is certainly an option, especially for uncomplicated pregnancies and births. It gives you the most control over the process, and it certainly provides a more familiar environment. Also, the cost can be significantly less than going to the hospital, and you avoid the issue of having to find someone to take care of the other kids. At home, you can take care of mom and the baby while still keeping an eye on your other children.

Most people who give birth at home have already gone through an uneventful pregnancy and delivery. You have to be confident of what you are doing, and you also have to be willing to take the risk that something could go wrong.

Birthing Center

More and more people are opting to have their babies in a birthing center. A birthing center takes a holistic approach to pregnancy and makes it more family centered. The birth usually involves a midwife delivering the baby, assisted by a physician. Birthing centers are generally meant for uncomplicated pregnancies and can be considered something of a compromise between giving birth in the hospital and having the baby at home.

Picking a Childbirth Class

When childbirth, or birthing, classes first became popular in the late 1960s and early 1970s, they were primarily designed as an alternative to traditional medicine and known as natural childbirth classes. The emphasis was on giving the parents more control and not using anesthetic medications. Although most birthing classes today still focus primarily on natural childbirth, there is an increasing emphasis on teaching parents-to-be what they can expect from traditional, clinical childbirth as well as such relevant health issues as prenatal care, nutrition, and exercise.

> **You should make time to attend all the birthing classes with mom. Not only will you learn a lot about labor and delivery, but the support you will be giving mom will mean a great deal to her.**

Lamaze

Developed by French obstetrician Dr. Fernand Lamaze, this technique espouses that the pain of childbirth can be overcome by focusing on something else—in this case the mother's own breathing. It is a variation of Ivan Pavlov's theory that learned reflexes can be overcome by repetition and training. Although it was principally developed as a method of natural childbirth, it can be used even if you and mom decide on using pain medications.

Bradley

Dr. Robert Bradley didn't like Lamaze's idea of distracting a woman from her pain. Instead, he thought she should overcome it by groaning or screaming as much as she wants. This is similar to what an athlete or a soldier might do to raise his adrenaline level before going into a game or a battle. This involves emphasizing natural breathing and muscle relaxation techniques as well as having the father play an integral role as the birth coach.

Leboyer

The Leboyer method was developed by French obstetrician Dr. Frederick Leboyer, who believed that babies should be born in a tranquil environment and with as little "violence" as possible. This technique usually involves dim lighting, soft music, and warm baths for the mother and the newly arrived baby. The traditional spanking, to get the baby crying and open the lungs, and quick cutting of the umbilical cord are discouraged.

Dick-Read

The technique developed by English obstetrician Dr. Grantly Dick-Read comes from the belief that fear leads to a "fight or flight" instinct, which results in adrenaline being released and blood being shunted away from the uterus and, thus, pain. His idea is that if you can get rid of the fear by whatever means, including relaxation techniques and hypnosis, then the pain will be diminished.

Selecting the Birth Team

Before the baby arrives, it is important to determine who is going to participate in the birth process and which person will make decisions. The most common arrangement is for the father to be present as a birth coach and be co–decision maker. However, many parents are choosing alternative arrangements.

Family Members

Some women prefer to have more family members present during the birth than just the father. Most commonly this refers to sisters or other female relatives, but it is not unheard of to have male relatives present as well. Also, some couples like to include their other children in the birthing process. Depending on the age and the maturity of the children, this can be a very positive bonding experience.

Doula

Although more and more men are acting as birth coaches, some women prefer to have another woman present. It is possible to hire a private labor assistant, or doula, to assist you and mom through the process. The doula doesn't replace the doctor, the licensed midwife, or you during the labor process. However, she can use her experience and training to give emotional support and offer advice to mom.

Doctors-in-Training

If you have decided to have your baby in a teaching hospital, mom may be taken care of by a doctor-in-training. They are usually referred to as medical students, interns, residents, or fellows. If mom is uncomfortable with this, she should talk to her doctor before she goes into labor. Many doctors and hospitals will insist that a doctor-in-training be allowed to participate because of their obligations or commitments to teaching.

Labor and Delivery Preferences

Many women imagine what their ideal childbirth entails. Although it is not always possible to choose every aspect of the birthing process, you and mom do have some choices. It is important to know, before mom goes into labor, whether her preferences conflict with the normal procedures of the facility and her health care provider. If they do conflict, she should talk to her doctor about her preferences beforehand.

Enemas

Many women are offered enemas to clear the stool from their colons before starting the pushing process. Although this can help alleviate the fear of having a bowel movement while pushing, it really isn't necessary. Passing stool during labor is relatively common and it is usually cleaned up very quickly and discreetly.

> It used to be standard practice for every woman to have her pubic hair shaved before the baby was delivered. Although some doctors feel that this helps them to visualize the birthing area better, it isn't really necessary, except in cesarean sections.

Intravenous Lines

It is often standard procedure to place an intravenous (IV) line in someone being admitted to the hospital. It makes it easy to prevent dehydration by giving fluids, and it allows for provision of intravenous medications if necessary. If mom is concerned about an IV line limiting her freedom, she can ask that it not be placed until necessary.

Bladder Catheters

Placement of a catheter in the bladder to remove urine is often performed when it is inconvenient or impossible for the woman to go to the bathroom. A catheter can also be used to keep track of the amount of urine she is making to see if she is getting dehydrated. Except during a cesarean section, a catheter may be unnecessary. It can place the woman at risk for complications from a urinary tract infection.

External Fetal Monitoring

Many women feel that having an external fetal monitor constantly hooked up to them is unnatural and intrusive. However, it is an important tool in making sure that the baby is safe. Although the mother can request that it be used less frequently, it is still important to have the baby monitored to make sure he is getting enough oxygen and is out of danger in other ways.

Eating and Drinking

It is very common for hospitals to restrict eating and drinking during labor. This is because of the concern that something might go wrong and the mother may need to undergo emergency surgery under general anesthesia. If this happens with a full stomach, it can lead to food aspiration into the lungs and serious infections. In most cases, requesting clear liquids during early labor and before the pushing has started is reasonable.

Episiotomy

It used to be standard practice for a doctor to perform an episiotomy during childbirth. The idea is that a small surgical incision in the birth canal can help make room for the baby's head and prevent a larger tear. Many women request that it not be done. However, if there is a high risk of a tear, they should leave it up to the judgment of their doctor.

More and more expectant fathers are interested in cutting the umbilical cord after the baby has come out. If this is something you want to do, you need to let the staff know. It may not always be possible, especially if the cord is wrapped around the baby's neck or mom is undergoing a cesarean section.

Pain Medications

Despite the fact that labor is an incredibly painful process, many women would like to use as little pain medication as possible. But because it is not uncommon for somebody to change her mind or to unexpectedly need such drugs for a medical reason, it is important to be aware of what the options are, why they are used, and what the pros and cons are.

Systemic Medications

Systemic medication involves injecting both narcotic (e.g., morphine, Demerol, or fentanyl) and nonnarcotic pain medications intravenously or intramuscularly. It is called systemic because the medication is not limited to a particular region of the body. The advantage is that it doesn't require placing a needle in or near the spine. However, it does have significant drawbacks, including drowsiness, nausea and vomiting, and low blood pressure. If the drugs are given too close to delivery, the baby may come out sleepy and, in some cases, have trouble breathing.

Epidural Anesthesia

An epidural is the most common form of pain control during childbirth. It involves placing a needle into the lower back and then threading a tiny plastic catheter near the spinal cord. Medications can then be injected to dull sensations from the lower spine, including nerve signals from the uterus, vagina, and perineum. An important advantage is that the medications can be introduced slowly and adjusted during labor.

Because an epidural needs to be placed by an experienced anesthesiologist and requires careful monitoring throughout the labor, it is not available everywhere. If mom is interested in getting one, she needs to make sure it is available at your hospital.

Spinal Anesthesia

Spinal anesthesia is similar to an epidural except that the medication is placed rapidly and all at once into the spinal fluid. Because it can knock out all sensations below the umbilical cord for two hours, it is usually reserved for cesarean sections.

Local Nerve Blocks

Occasionally, numbing medicine is used to block pain involving only the vagina and perineum and not that of the uterus contractions. The most common procedures are caudal block, saddle block, and pudendal block. The advantage is that the commencement of pain control is very quick and it doesn't affect the muscles. The disadvantage is that the anesthetics wear off quickly and don't help with contraction pain. Also, administering the caudal and saddle blocks requires significant skill and experience, which will not be available everywhere.

General Anesthesia

General anesthesia involves mom being completely knocked out, so that she is unconscious throughout the delivery. Although reasonably safe, it has a higher incidence of complications than epidural or spinal anesthesia. It is now used only in the case of an emergency, where there is no time to perform regional anesthesia or there is a contraindication for placing a needle in the spinal column. In this case, it's unlikely that you will have the luxury of discussing the risks and benefits, and the doctors will unilaterally make the decision.

There is increasing interest in alternative forms of pain control during labor. Some of the methods that are available include:
- Breathing or Lamaze
- Massage or reflexology
- Hydrotherapy and birthing balls
- Hypnosis and acupuncture

Assisting Labor and Delivery

Although having a baby is a natural process, it doesn't mean that it always runs smoothly on its own. Not infrequently, it is necessary for a doctor to step in and help things along.

Inducing Labor

There are a number of reasons why labor might be induced, but the most common are that the baby is post-due, the membranes are ruptured but labor hasn't started, or there is a condition where the baby and/or mother will be at risk if the pregnancy continues.

Ripening the Cervix

Placing prostaglandins into the vagina and next to the cervix can help start the process by dilating and thinning out the cervix. Medications such as Cervidil® or misoprostol are said to "ripen" the cervix.

Inflating the Cervix

Inflating the cervix occurs when the doctor inserts a catheter with a small, uninflated balloon (called a Foley catheter) into the cervix and then blows the balloon up. The pressure applied to the cervix can lead to the release of natural prostaglandins, which then cause the cervix to open and soften.

Breaking Her Water

Assuming that the cervix is somewhat dilated, it is possible to insert a small, plastic hooked instrument to rupture the amniotic sac. This may be enough to start the labor process by itself, but it is often used with uterine contraction stimulation as well. Once the process begins, the baby has to be delivered within 24 hours to minimize infections.

Starting Uterine Contractions

Using a synthetic form of a hormone called oxytocin (brand name Pitocin®), your doctor can cause labor contractions to start or increase in intensity and frequency. Oxytocin is the body's messenger to the uterus, telling it that it is time for labor.

Augmenting Labor

Sometimes labor starts but does not progress as well as it should. The use of oxytocin to help increase the strength, duration, or frequency of the contractions is the most common method of augmenting labor. Although it is generally safe, there is some risk that the contractions will be too intense and damage the uterus.

Assisted Delivery

Assisted delivery is also called operative vaginal delivery. If at some point it becomes apparent that the mother is too tired to push, spontaneous delivery becomes unlikely because the baby's position is wrong, or the baby's heart rate is of concern, the doctor can assist with the delivery. The two most common ways are by using forceps or a vacuum extractor. In either case, it requires that the baby be far enough along in the birth canal to make it through the pelvis. Used properly, these options can help avoid a cesarean section.

> Because of the pressure that forceps apply to the baby's head, it is common for the baby to have some scary-looking marks afterward. They go away in a couple of days and generally do not cause any long-term problems.

Forceps

Forceps are spatula-like instruments that curve in a way to fit around the sides of the baby's head. They are used to guide the baby through the birth canal. In the past, they caused serious harm if the baby was too high in the birth canal. Nowadays, forceps are used only when the baby is far enough along, so their use is much safer.

Vacuum Extractor

As the name suggests, a vacuum extractor attaches to the baby's head and sucks him out. It usually requires only a gentle pull. The doctor should not be yanking the baby out! However, it is common for the baby to have a round, raised area on his head that looks worse than it is, especially if there is a bruise. It will go away after a couple of days.

Cesarean Section

Sometimes it is not possible or safe to perform or continue normal delivery, and a cesarean section may have to be performed. Because of its high rate of use, some people are concerned that the procedure is being used for the physician's convenience rather than out of medical necessity.

Indications

A cesarean section is major surgery and should not be performed unless there is a clear medical reason. Although there are a number of reasons why a woman might end up having one, they generally fall into one of the following three categories.

Planned Cesarean

It is not uncommon for cesarean sections to be planned well in advance of the baby's arrival. The most common reasons for this include breech positioning, previous uterus surgery (including prior cesarean sections), placenta previa, and a pregnancy with three or more babies.

Unplanned Cesarean

There are a number of conditions that can arise during labor that are not emergencies but do necessitate a cesarean section. The most common reasons are arrested labor (not responding to medications) or problems with the baby's passage through the birth canal. Occasionally, a cesarean section may be performed if the baby is not tolerating labor.

Emergencies

Although rare, there are some conditions that require an immediate, emergency cesarean section to save the life of the baby or the mother. The most serious conditions are excessive bleeding, the umbilical cord preceding the baby, and prolonged slowing of the baby's heart rate, indicating poor blood flow and low oxygen.

> In some places today, C-sections are performed in 20–30% of births. This is dramatically higher than the rate two or three decades ago. To many, this very high rate of use indicates that C-sections are needlessly being utilized.

The Procedure

Cesarean section is a surgical procedure that requires a sterile operating room. Epidural, spinal, or general anesthesia is necessary to prevent pain. The doctor cuts through the skin, abdominal muscles, peritoneal cavity, and finally the uterus. The baby is removed, the bleeding controlled, and everything stitched up.

Risks and Complications

As with any surgical procedure, there is a risk of bleeding and infection. There is also a risk of injury to the bladder, bowel, or intestines, and other organs. Blood clots in the legs are another risk. Despite all this, the procedure is relatively straightforward and very safe. The benefit to the mother or the baby usually far outweighs any potential risk. However, if there is time to discuss the benefits and risks, it is still important to go over them with the doctor.

7

Getting Ready for Baby

Getting ready for the baby is very important to new mothers. They usually have strong opinions on what they want and plan accordingly. Expectant fathers may or may not have preferences on how they should prepare, but need to get involved either way. During this time, you will help get things ready for the baby, keep costs under control, and, more important, help address a number of safety issues.

Moving to a New Home

Many couples expecting their first child can suddenly feel like their home is too small. There can be a strong urge to go out and find a bigger and better home before the baby is born. Before deciding that you need to move, you should evaluate the benefits and the costs very carefully. This is especially important if you are thinking of buying a house for the first time.

Having More Space

Although babies are small, they have big needs. Initially, the baby may sleep in your bedroom, but eventually the little one is going to get bigger and will probably need a room of his own. If this means you are going to be losing a guest bedroom, a home office, or some other useful space to make room for a nursery, you might consider getting a bigger place. If you can afford it, a place where you can have a dedicated playroom to keep the toys from quickly spreading out through the home is a huge bonus.

Having a Decent-Size Yard

At first the baby won't be too mobile, but within a year he sure will be. Young kids have a lot of energy, and they need to get outside to run around and play. Having a place where your child can safely play is very important. Unless you already have a decent-size yard, or there is a park within walking distance, adequate room for your child to play outside is a good reason to consider moving.

Looking at the School District

Thinking about the school district you are living in may not seem like a concern since kindergarten is five or six years away. It should be, however. If you are already in a great school district, can you afford to stay in the area? You don't want to buy a bigger house with more land somewhere else, only to find out later that the school district is not very good. This is a particular issue in areas with a lot of new development but a lagging school infrastructure. It is a good idea to do preliminary research on school districts where you might live.

If you are considering buying a home, don't take the realtor's word that the schools are good. Look at the rankings yourself and, if possible, talk to parents whose children are in the system.

Proximity to Family

You may have heard from your friends or coworkers that once you start having children, it is very important to be close to other family. This is true. Not only is it good for the children to grow up knowing their relatives, but there will often be times when you will need the extra help. This is particularly true if both you and mom have demanding careers, or if one of you travels frequently. If you are thinking of moving more than an hour away from family, you may not know what you'll be missing!

Longer Commute

It is not uncommon for people to have difficulty balancing the type of home they want with what they can afford. As a result, they may decide to move to an area that is less expensive but farther away from where they work. Before trading a shorter commute for a bigger home, consider whether you might regret it later. If you already have a stressful or demanding job, think about how leaving earlier and coming home later will affect your family life. It may be better to have a smaller home but less stress in your life and more time for your child.

> Who drives the new car will depend a lot on your working situations. If mom is staying home, then it is obvious that she will need the bigger car. If both you and your wife work, and you are the one dropping the baby off at daycare, then you will need the bigger car.

Getting a New Car

Many expectant parents realize early on that their current vehicle is just not going to cut it when the baby is born. For many, the obvious choice is to get something larger.

Safety

In addition to extra room, safety has to be a top concern when looking for a new car. In general, the bigger the car, the better it will do in a crash. This is because a larger car will transfer more of its energy to the thing it hits in a crash. As a result, the car will decelerate less quickly. In addition, you should be looking for a well-designed car, with both front and side air bags, and a good reputation for safety.

New cars tend to drop in value within the first one or two years of ownership. If you think that you might be selling the car within a few years, it may make more economic sense to buy a used car.

Costs

When looking at the costs of a new car, you need to keep in mind potential finance charges, extra gas, higher insurance, and more costly maintenance. When these costs are taken altogether, a new car may be more expensive than you think.

Setting up the Nursery

When the baby is very young, he will probably be sleeping in a bassinet or playpen close by for convenience. After a couple of months, it is usually a good idea to move the baby to his own room. Not only does it help you and mom get a better night's sleep, it also helps establish a good sleeping routine for the baby. When setting up a nursery, there are a few pieces of furniture that most expectant couples consider buying.

Crib

The crib will be the place where the baby spends much of his time, and it is the single most important piece of furniture in the nursery. Unfortunately, new cribs are not cheap. A good crib can cost a lot, and that doesn't even include the cost of the mattress and bedding. Do some research, though, as some of the safest cribs are reasonably priced.

Design

Cribs manufactured after 1974 have to meet strict safety standards. The space between the slats should be no more than 2 ⅜ inches. The corner posts should be the same height as (or less than ⅟₁₆ inch higher than) the end panels. There should not be any cut out areas on the headboard or floorboard. The top rails of the sides should be at least 26 inches above the mattress set in its lowest position.

It is critical to realize that a crib is a potential hazard. Every year in the United States, tens of thousands of infants are hurt in unsafe cribs. Deaths from unsafe cribs can occur, though it is rare.

All new cribs purchased from reputable manufacturers are required to conform to certain safety requirements. Although buying a new crib doesn't guarantee that there won't be an accident, it makes it a lot less likely.

Location

When you're planning out the nursery, keep in mind that the crib should not be placed next to a window or under pictures or bookshelves. This is particularly important if you live in an area that tends to have earthquakes or severe storms.

Stability

The crib should be stable, and all nuts, screws, and other hardware should be solid, secure, and in place. The sides of the crib should be secure and should require either two distinct actions or significant pressure to open.

Surface

The hardware should be smooth and without sharp edges, points, or particularly rough surfaces. Anything broken, bent, loose, or disengaged needs to be fixed or replaced.

Not every couple can afford to purchase a new crib. In fact, a majority of newborns sleep in used cribs. Most of these used cribs comply with current safety regulations, but it is up to you to make sure. With a little bit of effort, you can get a safe crib at a reasonable discount.

Mattress

Most cribs require that you buy a mattress separately. It should be firm and flat, with no soft bedding underneath. It should fit snugly in the crib, and there should not be any gaps. If you can fit two or more fingers between the mattress and the crib, the mattress needs to be replaced. It should not be covered with anything plastic, such as mattress covers, to prevent suffocation. All this helps reduce the risk of suffocation and sudden infant death syndrome (SIDS).

Changing Table

A changing table is often just a dresser with a dedicated space for a foam rest where you can lay the baby while changing diapers. Since there is a good chance that you will be doing your share of diaper changing, you will appreciate having someplace high to do it, so you are not constantly bending over. Also, having all the supplies available and within easy reach takes some of the pain out of changing even the stinkiest diaper.

Rocking Chair or Glider

At some point it is likely that you will be feeding the baby in the middle of the night. Breast pumps make this possible even if mom is breastfeeding. Having a nice rocking chair, or better yet a glider, can make a 3 AM feeding a lot more tolerable. The rhythmic movement is comforting to the baby and gives you something to do too. Although rockers or gliders may not be cheap, for the sake of your back and arms, they can be worth it.

Decorations and Accessories

There are a lot of decoration and accessory options for a nursery. The ones most commonly purchased are bumper pads, pillows, stuffed animals, and mobiles. Keep in mind that when the baby is older and starting to roll, some of the accessories have to be removed for safety reasons.

Buying a Car Seat

A child car seat has become a necessary purchase when you have a new baby. Not only may it save the life of your child in a car accident, it is also required by law in every state. If you are pulled over by a police officer and you don't have one, you can expect to get a hefty fine.

Selecting a Car Seat

There are basically four types of car seats, but only two of them are appropriate for infants. At some point, of course, you will need to buy one of the other kinds as well.

Infant Only

An infant-only car seat is smaller and better suited for newborns. It is rear facing and can hold up to 20 pounds. Many are sold with detachable bases so that they can fit in strollers and shopping carts. The best have five-point restraints and tether straps.

Convertible

A convertible seat is designed for both newborns and young toddlers. It is initially rear facing for the infant less than 20 pounds, and it can be converted to forward facing when the baby gets older and heavier.

Forward Facing

A forward-facing seat is designed strictly for children heavier than 20 pounds but less than 30–40 pounds, depending on the manufacturer. The forward-facing car seat absolutely cannot be used for newborns or infants under 20 pounds.

Booster

A booster seat is designed for children over 30–40 pounds, depending on the manufacturer. It is designed to raise the child high enough to be able to safely use the car's standard seat belts.

Selecting a Brand

All new child car seats are required to meet certain minimum federal requirements. So in theory, any of the many car seats on the market should be safe. But in reality, some car seats are safer than others. Before selecting a brand, research its safety record.

> Not every car easily accommodates a car seat. Unless you are absolutely certain that you have placed the car seat in correctly, you should consider having it checked by a professional. It has been estimated that 80% of child car seats are not installed properly.

Installation

One of the hardest things about putting a car seat in is making sure it is properly secured. You have to make sure that not only the seatbelt is properly in place, but the additional securing lines are too. The car seat should always be placed in the backseat and away from air bags. Infants that weigh 20 pounds or less should be using a rear-facing infant seat.

Other Important Purchases

There are a number of items that you and mom will likely be looking at before the baby arrives. Mom may ask for your opinion on some of them, so it is a good idea to have at least considered the options.

Strollers

Initially it might be easy to carry the baby around in the car seat, but sooner or later you are going to have to get a stroller. Strollers are not cheap, so you want to think carefully about which of the different designs you want or need.

Carriage

The carriage stroller has a flat surface and is useful only while the baby is lying down. Carriage strollers used to be very popular, but aren't as much any more because of their limited life span. I would recommend against getting one of these.

> If you or mom is an avid jogger, you may want to consider getting a jogging stroller. This stroller has a heavier frame, shock absorbers, and special tires.

Reclining Stroller

The reclining stroller lives up to its name as it has the option of reclining. It acts like a carriage stroller in its flattest position, but it can adjust up as the baby grows and learns to sit up. It usually has a well-padded seat and backrest, so it is very comfortable for the baby.

Umbrella Stroller

An umbrella stroller is lightweight and easy to fold. It is great for traveling, but it isn't as comfortable and doesn't recline. It is relatively inexpensive but better for older infants.

Two-Seater Stroller

A two-seater stroller is great when you have twins or closely aged kids. You can get front-to-back or side-to-side seats. Each has its pros and cons. It is hard to justify buying it for just one baby, but if you are planning on another baby within the next couple of years, it may be worth it.

Baby Clothes

Beware: baby clothes are expensive! Unfortunately, because babies grow so quickly, they usually wear outfits for only a few months before they don't fit anymore. You and mom should have a baby clothes budget, just as you would for any other items.

Babies and small children outgrow most of their clothes before they have a chance to wear them out. With a little effort, you should be able to find some great bargains at consignment stores, garage sales, and even on eBay. Don't forget to ask friends and relatives if they have clothes that their children have outgrown.

Size

People buy clothes not based on how old the baby is at the moment but based on when the baby is going to wear them. Baby sizes are determined by age periods: newborn, 3–6 months, 6–12 months, and 12–18 months, for example. If your baby is smaller or larger than the average for his age group, it is important to let would-be gift givers know the appropriate size, not just the baby's age.

Colors

Clothing styles for newborns and young babies are fairly gender neutral. It is the colors that can distinguish whether something is for a boy or for a girl. (Everybody knows that blue is for a boy and pink is for a girl, right?) Neutral but bright colors such as yellow or green could go either way. If you and mom aren't planning on finding out the sex before your baby is born, neutral colors may be a good way for you to go—for the clothes *and* the nursery.

Quality

Not all baby clothes are of the same quality. Although a high price increases the odds of getting something better made, it doesn't guarantee it. Check with mom before making any purchases—this will save you from having to return items that are the wrong brand or material.

Portable Cribs

Young babies can be easier to travel with than older ones. They tend to sleep much of the time, so early on you may feel more comfortable flying or going out to dinner. If you travel and you are not staying in a hotel, you are going to need a portable crib. These cribs are also nice to place in another part of the home, to be able to put the baby down for a nap in the middle of the day.

Intercom

Many parents feel uncomfortable closing the door and leaving the baby unattended for a nap. Having an intercom is a great way to know when the baby is awake or if he's restless. An intercom is essentially a one-way walkie-talkie that is always on. Although you can get a video version, it probably isn't necessary or worth the cost.

Diaper Pail

Unless your baby is getting formula, the diapers won't be too stinky to begin with. Sooner or later, however, they will start to get a bit powerful. Since you don't want to have to run outside every time the baby has a poopy diaper, having something to put them in is important. Among the products for disposal out there are a number of systems that are designed to form a seal. They are costly and require a lot of refills, but you will come to appreciate it.

Bouncy Seat

A bouncy seat is a type of baby holder that typically reclines and has a battery-powered vibrator and/or music machine. The baby is strapped in and slightly reclined. This seat was particularly helpful in getting our newborns to relax. It is also a good way of getting mom to put down the baby and relax herself.

Baby Swing

Although the newborn baby will be too small to be in a swing, pregnancy is a good time to think about getting one. They are relatively inexpensive and very useful. The swinging motion can keep a fussy baby content for hours.

8

Money and Finances

Money is necessary to obtain basic necessities such as food, housing, clothes, personal hygiene products, and health care. To get your finances in order, you need to start analyzing your financial health, determining areas of attention, and then developing a plan of action. Your goal is to be able to provide the basics, protect against catastrophic loss, and then start saving for long-term goals like owning a home, financial independence, retirement, or college. Key to this is avoiding overspending or buying on credit, not making decisions based on temporary emotions, and doing your homework. While doing all this, it is important that you don't become so obsessed with money that you become stressed out and miserable.

High Cost of Raising a Child

Brace yourself. Based on the latest data from the government, you can expect to pay over $250,000 to raise a child from birth through age 17. Of course, this is just an average estimate and the true cost will depend a lot on your income, lifestyle, and the number of children you have. It doesn't include unusual medical bills, private school or college, or the loss of income if one parent reduces work hours, stops working, or takes a lower-paying job. However, it does give you a rough sense of the costs and helps explain why people are having smaller families now than they used to. Regardless of what it actually costs, the benefit you get from having children is priceless.

Housing

Having a baby may make your cozy apartment or house unbearably cramped. The cost of moving can be substantial, especially if you decide to go from renting to owning, as this can mean a large down payment. It is estimated that additional living space is the single biggest expense of raising children, ranging from $45,000 to $100,000. However, this assumes that you are going to add an additional 100 to 150 square feet of living space to your home, either through renovating your existing home or buying a new one. Not everyone wants to, needs to, or will increase the size of their home. But for those who do upgrade, the costs can be substantial.

> Reduce additional housing expenses by staying put for several months, moving to a less expensive area, and claiming tax deductions for mortgage interest, property taxes, or a home office. Also consider challenging your property tax and improving the energy efficiency of your current home.

Food

It is estimated that it costs between $26,000 and $39,000 to feed a child until he is 17. The cost of food during the first year may not be as much if mom is breastfeeding; however, if you're bottle feeding either as a supplement or for complete nourishment, the costs can be substantial. Joining warehouse clubs such as Sam's Club, Costco, or

BJ's can help, but sometimes you end up buying more than you would otherwise. Even if you are able to buy in bulk, you can expect to go through $100–$150 per month in formula alone.

Transportation

You would think that something so small wouldn't cost much to transport around. Good car seats are not cheap, but they are worth every penny. When the government estimates that it costs between $19,000 and $35,000 per child in transportation costs, it is including the purchase or finance charges of vehicles, repair and fuel expenses, and insurance. Obviously, until your child is old enough to drive, buying a single minivan will do, but they are certainly not cheap. Unless you have the money, you shouldn't buy a new car. The value of a new car drops dramatically in the first two years of owning it. Look for a used car that is only a couple of years old and still on its original warranty. Don't forget to take a look at your car insurance. It can vary widely among different companies, and you may be able to save money by comparing policies.

Some of the best used car deals can be found in the classifieds, but that can also be a big risk. If you are willing to take the chance, be sure to have the car checked by a mechanic you trust. Otherwise, you should consider a used car dealership.

Clothing

If you haven't seen the cost of children's clothes lately, you are in for a shock. The government estimates it costs between $8,500 and $13,000 to provide clothing for a child through the age of 17. Key to keeping costs down are not buying designer clothes, shopping during sales or looking for discounts, and buying clothes that can be shared among siblings.

Health Care

The government estimates that it costs between $11,000 and $16,000 to provide health care for a child through age 17. This can be very misleading and really depends on your insurance coverage and the health of the child. You most likely shoulder an increasing percentage of the insurance costs at work by paying part, if not all, of the premium, deductibles, and co-pays. Dental and vision may be separate or may not be covered at all. If you have no insurance or your child has a costly illness, your out-of-pocket costs can be staggering and potentially catastrophic.

> **An increasing number of companies are offering health savings accounts, which let you set aside pretax dollars for health care expenses. If you are self-employed, 100% of your health insurance costs may be deductible.**

Childcare

The government estimates that it costs between $12,000 and $34,000 per child for childcare expenses through age 17. Obviously, this depends on your situation. It doesn't include the loss of income if one of you quits and stays home to raise the children. Also, if both of you work, and you need full-time daycare, the cost is going to be substantially higher, especially if you have a nanny. Hiring a nanny could cost you that amount in a single year. There is some tax relief, but it doesn't cover everything.

Miscellaneous

Personal-care items, hobbies, entertainment, education, gifts, and other miscellaneous item are estimated to cost between $13,000 and $32,000 through age 17, but it depends on your lifestyle. If your child is going to have the best of everything, including private school, multiple one-on-one lessons (for music, tennis, martial arts, etc.), the most expensive toys, and the best vacations, then you can expect to pay much more. However, it is possible to save money and not affect the quality of your child's life by spending modestly and doing things yourself.

Tax Benefits of Having Children

To help offset all the extra expenses that you are going to have, there are some tax benefits for having children.

Personal Exemption

A child is considered a personal exemption, which reduces the amount of your earnings that are taxed. For 2006 the exemption was $3,300, and it is expected to increase by around $100 per year. For example, if in 2007 you had $50,000 in taxable income, it is estimated that having a baby will reduce your taxable income to $46,600. Because personal exemptions only reduce the amount of income you have to pay taxes on, the amount you save depends on your tax rate. For example, if you are in the 15% tax bracket, then for every $1 you get in deductions, you save only 15 cents.

If you need a more realistic idea of how the baby is going to change your tax bill, you could run a simulation using one of the commercial tax preparation software programs. By entering different scenarios into the software and calculating the taxes owed, you will get a more realistic estimate of the effect on your taxes, net pay, and cash flow.

Tax Credits

Unlike exemptions or deductions, a tax credit reduces your tax bill directly. This means that for every $1 you get in tax credits, you are cutting $1 off of your tax bill. In most cases, you benefit from a tax credit only if you owe taxes, but not always.

You can receive a tax credit up to $1,000 per child depending on your income level. It is limited if your income is above a certain point. If you are going to be paying for childcare so that you and your partner can work, you may also be able to get a portion of it back through this credit. Unfortunately, the credit is only a percentage of your expenses, and there is a cap. Also, to claim this credit, the person or company providing the care needs to have a tax identification number.

Flexible Spending Accounts

Flexible spending accounts are an employer-sponsored program that allows you to pay for childcare and medical costs using pre-tax dollars. This means that the amount of money you put in this account is subtracted from your taxable income. It acts as a deduction and not a credit. There is usually a cap of around $5,000, but it can be lower depending on how your company has it set up. Also, if you don't use all of it by the end of the year, your company—not you—can keep what's left over.

Analyzing Your Spending

The money that you might get back by reducing your taxes is not going to be nearly enough to cover the costs of raising a child. For most people, cutting down on expenses is a more effective approach to making ends meet. In order to do that, you first need to get a good handle on your spending. The best way to do that is to keep track of your expenses closely. Although not necessary, it is very helpful to use one of the many financial software packages available. To effectively track your expenses, you need to choose your expense categories wisely. The key is to be detailed yet simple. You can use the following expenses categories as a guide.

Taxes

You might not consider paying taxes as a spending category, but it is. It is important to realize how much you are paying, because you have some control over it through tax deductions and credits. To check this, you should look at your end-of-year W2 form and tax return from the previous year.

> Be careful to not get overly detailed or obsessive when tracking your expenses. Otherwise, you might find it too time-consuming and then lose interest. Remember that when you are trying to figure out where your money is going, you want to concentrate on the big picture.

Federal

Federal income tax is often the biggest tax you will be paying. How you pay obviously depends on the amount and type of your income, whether it be salary, dividends, or capital gains, as well as your deductions, such as mortgage interest, taxes paid, or charity donations and credits. Paying attention to potential deductions and credits is important to saving money.

State/Local

Your state and local taxes may be determined in the same way as your federal tax, but they are usually less. Each state does it a little bit differently, especially with respect to special deductions and credits. Some states do not have an income tax, and not every city has a local income tax.

Social Security

The government collects 12.4% of your salary for Social Security. You usually pay half and your employer pays half. If you are self-employed, you have to pay the entire 12.4%. Unlike federal and state income taxes, you can't reduce the amount you owe through deductions or credits. At the present time, only the first $94,200 of your salary is taxed.

Medicare

The government collects 2.9% of your salary for Medicare. Similar to Social Security, you pay only half (1.45%) unless you are self-employed. However, unlike Social Security, there is no cap on the amount you can owe.

Housing

For most people, housing is their biggest expense. If you rent, determining the amount you spend is pretty straightforward. However, if you own your own home, it can be a little more complex. Even though you might be sending the bank one check a month, it usually covers several different expenses. Those expenses that aren't paid every month are held aside.

> Often, the biggest part of a mortgage payment is for interest on the loan. Fortunately, the interest is usually tax deductible.

Mortgage Principal

A certain amount of your mortgage payment goes toward paying off the loan balance (i.e., the principal). This amount isn't tax deductible, but it does consistently increase your equity in your home.

Private Mortgage Insurance (PMI)

Many banks used to require a down payment equal to 20% of the cost of the home. Those who couldn't afford that could purchase private mortgage insurance (PMI) to protect the bank or mortgage company against a default. This usually adds several hundred dollars to the monthly mortgage payment. During the recent run-up in housing prices, however, the PMI wasn't always required.

Property Tax

Your local government taxes your home and property using a percentage of their assessed value. Many banks or mortgage companies will facilitate the payment of the tax to help prevent missed payments and liens being placed on the property. In this case, the money is bundled as part of the mortgage payment and thus collected every month. Because property taxes are paid only once or twice a year, this money is held in escrow until it is time to pay.

Homeowners Insurance

In order to get a mortgage, you need to have homeowners insurance to protect against catastrophic loss. If you live in an area prone to flooding, a special policy obtained through the government is usually required. Many banks or mortgage companies will place money in escrow (similar to property tax) and use it to pay a yearly premium.

Association Fees

If you live in a condominium or other community that has shared responsibility for property upkeep and security, you probably are required to join a homeowners association. Fees are usually assessed monthly and can easily run into hundreds of dollars.

Home Maintenance

If you own your home, you are responsible for its maintenance and repairs, including yard maintenance, tree trimming, gutter cleaning, and other outside chores. There is no landlord you can call at the first sign of trouble, and these expenses can really add up. Major infrequent and unpredictable repairs (such as a broken dishwasher) should be included elsewhere. You should also not include payments for a cleaning person or service here.

Basic Living Expenses

There are many ways to categorize and subcategorize basic living expenses. This section should include basic necessities; luxuries or other extras should be included in the discretionary section below. Sometimes it can be hard to decide if something is a basic necessity or a luxury (for example, cable television or a cellular phone). If you can live without it in a pinch, put it in the discretionary section.

Food

Include groceries that you purchase at the store and eat at home or bring to work as a basic expense. The reason not to include eating out is that it is expensive and something of a luxury. You may or may not want to include lunches, such drinks as coffee and alcohol, and snacks here.

> Eating out may not seem like a luxury to you now, but it may when the baby arrives. When you find that dinner at your favorite restaurant costs as much as one month's supply of diapers, you might decide that you don't need to go out as often.

Household

General household expenses include personal-care products, cleaning products, bedding, and other things regularly needed to keep a home going. This does not include art and other nonfunctional purchases.

Utilities

Utilities include gas, electricity, heating oil, water, sewer, and phone, as well as cellular phones, cable television, and Internet access. Some people consider the last few to be luxuries, whereas others view them as basics.

Transportation

If you own a car, the costs include auto insurance, gasoline, and such maintenance as oil changes, tune-ups, and tire replacement. You should also include repairs, tolls, parking, and registration costs, if applicable. Auto loan expenses should be included in the debt section, not here. If you have a car lease that isn't reimbursed by your company, you can include it here. If you don't drive, this might include paying for public transportation.

Medical

An increasing number of employers and insurance companies are shifting the cost of health care to employees. You should include such costs as insurance premiums, deductibles, co-pays, medications, dental work, and vision care. Keep in mind that costs related to the pregnancy are going to cause medical expenses to temporarily spike.

Additional Insurance

If you have any insurance payments in addition to homeowners, auto, and medical, add them here. This typically includes life insurance, disability insurance, and personal article insurance. Don't include insurance that is paid for by your employer.

Childcare

If this is your first child, you obviously won't have any other, preexisting childcare expenses; otherwise include those. If you have a nanny, include her salary, bonuses, your share of Social Security and Medicare taxes, as well as the cost of unemployment insurance.

> **Make sure to include clothing in your list of expenses. This includes both business and casual clothes, as well as the clothes of your other kids. Dry cleaning costs should also be included.**

Education

If either you or mom is still in school or involved in advancing or changing your career, include all the costs here. If you are taking courses for enrichment or other reasons, include this cost under hobbies. If you have children who are enrolled in school (public or private), include the costs here.

Discretionary Expenses

What is considered discretionary depends on who you ask. This section is designed to identify some expenses that certainly can add richness to your life, but may not be absolutely necessary. Also, identify and exclude business expenses that are fully reimbursed.

Eating Out

Include meals out that could be easily replaced by eating at home. This clearly includes going out to restaurants in the evenings or on weekends. Whether you want to include breakfasts, lunches, and snacks is up to you.

Cleaning

Do you hire someone to come to your home and clean? If both of you are working and have little free time, it makes sense to have a cleaning service. However, with having to spend more time at home with the baby comes the opportunity to do your own cleaning and save some money.

Entertainment

You might be surprised at how much money you spend on entertainment, especially if you don't have kids. Again, with a new baby, you may not have the time and energy to maintain a busy social life.

Sports/Hobbies

Do you spend a lot of money playing golf or other sports? Do you have some cool but not inexpensive hobbies? Tally some of those costs. It may be something of a sacrifice, but perhaps there is an opportunity to spend more modestly in this area. However, you should hold the line on some key activities, especially if you are passionate about them. If you sacrifice too much here, the subconscious resentment may outweigh any benefits of saving the money.

Vacations and Travel

For a young couple without kids, travel can account for a large part of discretionary spending. Early on, when the baby is small, you will still be able to travel, but as he gets older, you won't be quite so flexible, and you should plan your vacations more carefully. Additional airfare and a larger hotel room size will be factors in your planning.

Gifts

It is certainly true that it is better to give than to receive. Sometimes we think that paying a lot for a gift gives it more meaning. But sometimes we pay too much because we wait until the last minute and are desperate. In either case, by planning ahead and being thoughtful, there is an opportunity to save on expenses and actually improve the quality of your gifts.

Miscellaneous

There are so many small expenses that it can be impossible to keep track of them unless you vigilantly enter them into a financial planner of some sort. To get an idea of your miscellaneous expenses, especially when using cash, it is a good idea to keep track of them in a small notebook for a month. By doing so, you will realize how much you are spending as well as identifying potential areas for saving.

Debt

This section applies to non-mortgage debt. Unlike mortgage debt, your goal should be to pay off all of your debt as soon as possible. Consumer debt can breed insecurity. It may temporarily give you pleasure to be able to able to buy something you want, but it ultimately comes at a cost—unhappiness and insecurity. You may become unhappy because you are required to work longer and harder, possibly to pay for something you may not have been able to afford in the first place. You may become insecure because you have limited control of your finances and more susceptible to unexpected expenses.

Credit Cards

When calculating credit card debt, separate the finance charges, interest, and penalties from the principal or original cost. Although you want to pay off the original debt too, you should have that source of debt under a separate category.

Auto Loans

Similar to credit card debt, there is a finance charge for a car loan. In the early part of the loan, you are paying primarily interest, but as you get closer to the end, you are paying more and more of the principal. You should calculate the amount of interest remaining on the loan and thus how much you could save if you paid it off sooner rather than later. Most auto loans let you pay off early, but check to be sure.

Student Loans

Although the cost of a student loan can be less than other debt (due to lower interest rates and potential tax deductions), it still has a finance charge. As with an auto loan, you should obtain the payout amount and determine the amount of interest remaining. If the rates are low and fixed, it may or may not make sense to pay it off more quickly, depending on your circumstances.

Other Debt

Other debts may include lines of credit, either secured with collateral (such as a home) or unsecured. They are usually tied to short-term interest rates. Even if they may be used as a tax deduction, give serious thought to paying them off as soon as possible. These could also include repayment of personal loans to family, friends, or another person or organization.

Savings

Although you might not consider savings an expense, technically it is. You are taking some of the money and, instead of buying an object or a service, you are buying security and ultimately peace of mind.

Retirement

In this category, include only contributions to retirement accounts that you make. Don't include matching contributions by your employer.

College

For college expenses, include only those contributions that are specifically designed for college or an educational fund. If there is no pretax advantage, or it is an account to which you have immediate and unrestricted access, consider it investment savings. This may apply only if you already have children, unless you are contributing to a college fund.

> Most retirement contributions have some sort of tax advantage that allows you to reduce the amount of taxes you owe. Unless you are starved for cash, it is always a good idea to contribute the maximum amount allowed to your retirement account.

Savings/Investments

You should be setting aside a certain amount of money as an emergency fund that will provide from 3 to 12 months of living expenses. This money should be relatively safe and accessible. It should not be put in high-risk investment accounts. If you are setting aside money for investing, be sure to pay off your other debt first. Don't be tempted by the logic that you can hold lower-interest debt and then earn higher-interest returns by investing it. Except for paying your rent or mortgage, setting aside for retirement, and funding your emergency savings, use any extra money that you don't need in the near future to pay off your debt as fast as possible.

Getting Extra Money

It is not uncommon when having your first baby to experience a temporary episode of being cash poor, even after cutting back expenses. A lot of this has to do with limited savings, significant medical expenses, and large one-time purchases to get ready for the baby. If at all possible, you want to avoid having to generate too many high-interest loans, such as with credit cards or nonsecured lines of credit. The following are some options for generating extra cash to cover these costs.

Selling Assets

Selling off something you own may be preferable to getting deeper in debt. Selling such assets as stocks and bonds may make sense, if they are not in retirement accounts. However, if you sell for a gain, you must remember to set aside enough money to pay the taxes. The selling of other property (e.g., a car) may not be worth it if it has depreciated and you can't get much for it, especially if you might need it in the future and would be forced to buy a replacement at a higher price.

Vesting Stock Options

Many companies offer stock options in lieu of a larger salary. Unless it is a near certainty that your options are above water and you are able to vest them, you should forget about them for now.

Home Equity Loans

With interest rates relatively low, it might be tempting to use the equity in your house to take out a loan. The interest rate is generally lower because it is secured by your house, and the interest may be tax deductible. However, since most home equity loans are tied to short-term interest rates, they can rise suddenly. With increasing rates and decreasing real estate prices, you should try to avoid these if you can. They are still preferable to unsecured loans and credit card debt, however.

Personal Loans

As a rule, borrowing from family and friends is a bad idea. But if the need is great, it is better than using credit cards. It is a good idea to set an appropriate interest rate and put everything down in writing. Even though you might consider it a loan, be sure to use the money wisely. If you don't, it can definitely lead to bad feelings.

Gifts

Many parents or soon-to-be grandparents are willing to help with the costs of starting a new family. They realize that with housing prices so high and the cost of living out of control, the younger generation needs more help. If you have a hard time accepting help from your relatives, just remember that they are helping your baby too, not just you.

Analyzing Your Credit

Young families just starting out often need to borrow money to buy a house or a car, or to pay for other baby expenses. Your ability to get a loan with a good interest rate will be determined in large part by your credit history and rating.

Getting Your Credit Report

You actually have three different credit reports, one for each of the major credit bureaus: Experian, Equifax, and TransUnion. In addition to personal identifying information, your report contains details on each credit account you have opened, including when it was opened, if there is a balance, the payment history (including late payments), and if it is still active. It also contains information on previous bankruptcy filings and requests for your credit report. In theory, each of the three reports should contain the same information, but in reality, there can be significant differences or mistakes. So, it is probably worth your time to review all three.

Knowing Your Credit Score

From the details in your credit reports, you are assigned a three-digit rating called a FICO (Fair Isaac Corporation) score. The FICO score ranges from 300 to 850. Those with lower scores have a much higher chance of defaulting on a loan or an obligation. Those with low credit scores can expect to pay finance charges, assuming they even get a loan. A FICO score below 620 is not considered good, and a score below 500 is considered very risky. On the other hand, a score above 620 is good, and a score above 700 is great.

Improving Your Credit Score

For good or bad, your credit score can have important implications for whether you receive a loan and how high the interest rate will be. It is also increasingly being used for screening potential renters and job applicants. Therefore, even if you don't plan on borrowing much in the future, it is important to improve your score whenever possible. The quickest way to do this is to make sure the information is accurate and that missed or late payments over seven years old are removed. After that, be sure to pay all your bills on time, reduce your debt, and avoid opening new credit card accounts.

Protecting Your Credit

Identity theft is on the rise, and someone who steals your identity can quickly destroy your credit. It is important to protect your Social Security number at all costs. Destroy unnecessary financial records and credit card offers by shredding them. It is important to monitor your credit reports periodically. Many companies offer identity fraud alert programs, but they can be expensive. A better approach may be to place a fraud alert with the credit bureau to prevent someone from opening a credit account without you being notified.

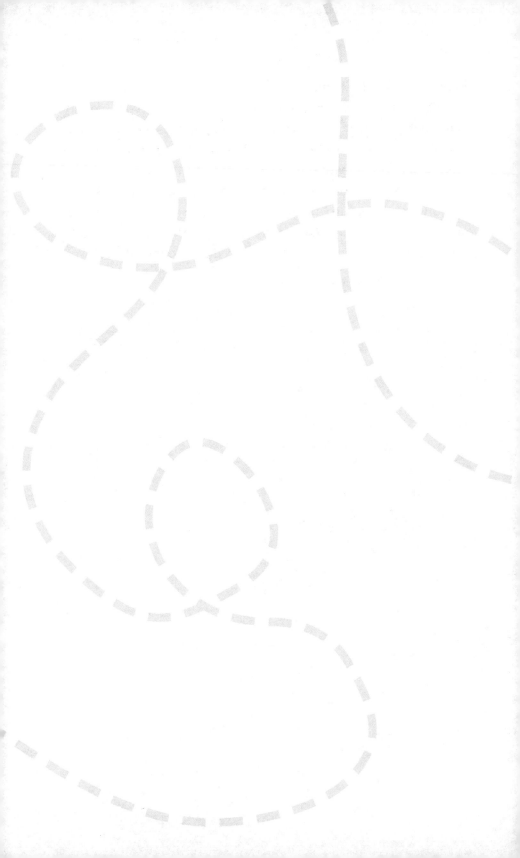

9

Work, Careers, and Childcare

Having a baby can dramatically change the way you think about your work and your career. The most immediate consideration is obvious if both of you are working. Before the baby is born, you will need to decide if one of you will stay home to take care of the baby or whether you will need daycare. Even if the childcare issues are settled, you will find that starting a family can cause you to reevaluate your job and career aspirations.

Assessing Your Current Job and Career

Before the baby arrives, it is important for you and mom to have a good idea of what is important for your family life and how your jobs will add to or detract from it. If you are not sure, you need to make a detailed assessment of your current job and career.

Income
When you are starting a new family and thinking about all the additional expenses, there is a tendency to fixate on the need to make more money. Study after study has shown that past a certain point,

making more money doesn't necessarily translate into happiness and a good family life. Of course, it is important to be able to provide the necessities for your family, but as they say, money isn't everything. If you go through and estimate your current and future expenses, you will get a rough idea of how much money you need to make. Beyond that, you need to consider other, non-monetary factors and how they are going to affect your family.

> Quitting one job for another, or changing a career when you are about to start a family, can have very serious consequences, but it may end up being one of the best decisions you made for your family.

Benefits

Before the baby came along, you might not have given much thought to insurance and retirement. But now you should. Most people obtain their health, dental, life, and disability insurance, as well as fund their retirement, through the company they work for. Although that arrangement is not necessary, it is in many ways easier and less expensive. Does your company offer good health, dental, life, and disability insurance? What about a retirement plan? If they don't, you need to consider buying insurance yourself or changing companies. At the other extreme, the benefits may be so good that it can make it difficult to go to another company that doesn't offer similar group benefits, especially if you have preexisting medical conditions. This may keep you in a job that you might not like.

Stability

Having a family makes it more important to have a stable job. When you were young, single, and without many obligations, you could afford to have unstable income or benefits. With a baby on the way, working for a larger, slower, and less exciting company for a salary and benefits may offer your family more stability than working at a young startup company for stock options. But if both you and your partner plan on working, it could be possible to have one of you in a stable job while the other pursues something less secure but with more potential. The key is that at least one of you has a stable and secure job.

Job Requirements

When you have a demanding job or career and no significant obligations outside of work, it can be easy to put your personal life on hold. If you and your partner both have demanding careers, you might even have found a way to make it all work. But in either case, now that you have a baby on the way, things are going to change. Unlike your partner, who might accommodate the demands of your job, a baby will not. Hoping or expecting others to compensate or cover for you at your job is probably not going to work in the long run. Thus, it is very important to evaluate the requirements of your job and career.

If there is a serious possibility that one of you might be quitting or changing your job or career after the baby is born, then you really need to start talking about it right away. It may take a lot of time and research to effectively plan what you're going to do, and the baby will arrive before you know it!

How much time does your job require? Are you working 60-, 80- or 100-hour work weeks? Do you know? For a month, keep track of how much time you spend commuting to and from the office, working at the office, and working at home. It's also important to consider how flexible your job is. Unless the number is extreme, measuring the total hours that you work doesn't tell you the whole story. Having children makes life less predictable. You can't control when they get sick or when something unexpected needs to be taken care of right away. A job with flexibility can make a big difference in those unexpected moments.

Jobs that involve a lot of traveling can also place stress on the family. Extended trips can be particularly hard on them. For many positions, traveling is one of the job requirements, but before the baby comes, you might think about ways to travel less.

Personal Satisfaction

A lot of careers pay very well but may not provide much personal satisfaction. Unfortunately, stress and unhappiness caused by work rarely stay at work. All too often they lead to impatience and frustration at home. Not only does this affect you, but it also affects everyone around you. Rationalizing that the extra money can make up for the stress by providing your family with more of the "finer things in life" is unhelpful. More money doesn't necessarily lead to sustained personal satisfaction from a job.

Effects of Changing Your Job

Unless both you and your partner have jobs or careers that you want or need to continue after the baby is born, you are likely to have a conversation about whether one of you should cut back or quit. With many couples, there is a large difference in earning capacity as well as in the desire to work. Traditionally, it has been common for the woman to quit and stay home. However, with more women developing thriving careers, it is not uncommon for couples to have similar earning potential and interest in their careers.

> There is an increasing trend for women to have better career potential than their partners. As a result, it is becoming more common for a man to make a change in his job or career so she can pursue hers.

Cash Flow

It isn't always clear what the effect of lost income will be on a family's cash flow and net worth. What might be lost in income may be made up for by saving on expenses and taxes. For example, if one of you stays home, there won't be the additional expenses of childcare, transportation, eating out, and other work-related, non-reimbursable expenses. The effect on taxes can be even harder to predict because of child-related tax deductions and credits that may now be available to you, as well as a potential lowering of your tax bracket because of the drop in your family income. To help assess your potential tax saving, you should consult a qualified tax accountant or run a simulation using one of the many available tax preparation software programs. To run a tax simulation, you should enter last year's tax information into the program. After entering potential changes to your income as well as anticipated childcare expenses, you will get a pretty good idea of how much you are going to save on taxes.

> Be sure to consider benefits carefully if you or mom are considering any career changes. Unfortunately, many of the benefits available through group plans at work are difficult to get individually. Keep this in mind if you are able to get family benefits only through one of your jobs.

Damage to Career

Certain careers can withstand a temporary pause, whereas others cannot. Although society is more tolerant of women taking time off to raise kids, it is still often perceived as putting your family before your career. Some people feel that this is a problem, but accepting these limitations sometimes improves not only your family life but also your personal sense of happiness.

Being Isolated

Transitioning from business employee to stay-at-home parent can be very isolating. Your main company for much of the day is a baby with very limited conversation skills. Many mothers will band together to form play dates, not only for their baby's socialization but for theirs as well. Since the number of men staying home is relatively small, there aren't as many socialization options as there are for women. If you are thinking of staying home, you have to consider the potentional for isolation.

Working with More Time off or Greater Flexibility

If you and your partner both need or want to continue working, one of you might consider looking for a career option with more time off or greater flexibility.

Traditionally, women have been more interested in exploring these career choices, but more and more men are considering them. This is especially true if the woman has a career with a higher earning potential.

Part-Time Work

With some jobs it's possible to reduce your responsibilities to part-time. Some companies see it as being to their advantage because they stop covering part of your salary and probably most of your expensive benefits, such as health insurance. They may not allow you to continue to participate in their retirement plan as well.

Telecommuting

With advances in technology, it has become easier to do productive work away from the office. Not only do you save time by not having to commute, you aren't under the watchful eyes of others, so you can take care of personal errands more easily. The problem is that it can be harder to motivate yourself at home, and you can be more easily distracted. Friends and family may assume that you aren't really working and that they can interrupt you more easily or more frequently. However, if you do it right, you will gain both flexibility and productivity. Your employer will like the idea of increased productivity and lower overhead expenses, but may have a concern that too many people will want to do it.

Starting Your Own Business

Another possibility is starting your own business by becoming a consultant to your current employer and others. Not only is there flexibility, there are pretty good tax advantages as well. The downside is that you will be responsible for taking care of your own taxes, including Social Security and Medicare, and benefits. Getting health insurance and setting up a retirement plan are also no easy tasks. You should consider this only if you are very independent, you are not sensitive to risk, and you can charge rates high enough to make up for the extra payroll taxes, potentially higher benefit costs, and loss of company matching for retirement. Also factor in what would happen if your old company decides to terminate its relationship with you. Can you find enough other business to survive?

> Starting your own business can be very rewarding and offer greater flexibility, but it can also be very stressful. There can be a lot of overhead costs in setting up your own office, and the income may not be as stable as you think. Starting your own business while having a new baby may turn out to be too stressful.

Maternity Leave

If mom decides to go back to work after having the baby, she will need to take maternity leave. Maternity leave can be a very sensitive subject. Nobody doubts the importance of maternity leave, but it can invoke strong emotions in both men and women. For example, expectant mothers can feel guilty about returning to work too early and may feel adamant about taking as much time as they can. On the other hand, co-workers may subconsciously harbor feelings of jealousy or resentment if they feel like she is taking "too much" time. In any case, in order to assess her options, mom will need to find out the maternity policy of her employer. The three key aspects of maternity leave are eligibility, duration, and if it is paid or unpaid.

Eligibility

Not every employer is obligated to offer maternity leave. Under the Family and Medical Leave Act of 1993, employees can to take up to 12 weeks of unpaid leave for the birth and care of a child. It also applies to new parents of an adopted child. The law applies to government agencies, public schools, and private companies with 50 or more employees. To be eligible, you or mom has to have worked at a company for at least one year and a total of 1,250 hours.

Although many employers are obligated to offer up to 12 weeks of maternity leave, they are not required to offer it with pay. They are required only to maintain the employee's health coverage and protect her position, unless they can prove "substantial and grievous economic injury." Be sure to plan accordingly if you are expecting a loss of income for 12 weeks.

Short-Term Disability

Many companies have short-term disability policies that can supplement mom's income once she is no longer able to work. Pregnancy can be considered a disability and typically starts when a physician certifies that she is no longer able to work. In most cases, the disability coverage stops after six weeks. Coverage beyond this usually requires a physician certification of continued disability.

Childcare

In the past, it was common for a woman to quit her job or career and stay home to take care of the children. The father continued to dedicate himself to advancing his career and earning money. Economically and socially this might have worked then; it was expected that the woman would stay home, and a family could do well on a single salary. Nowadays, things are very different.

Many women have more opportunities to pursue higher-paying and better careers. It can no longer be assumed that a man has the better or more stable job. Also, dramatic increases in the cost of living, particularly housing, often make it necessary for both parents to work. Thus, even if a woman wanted to quit her job and stay home, she may not be able to.

If you and your partner both want to or have to work, you are not alone. It is becoming increasingly common for both parents to be working, so finding good childcare is critical. In most places school doesn't start until kindergarten, but there are early childcare and preschool options.

> A generation ago, it was possible to afford a decent home on a single salary. Nowadays, the cost of housing is so high that many families need a dual income just to make ends met.

In-Home Care

If possible, most people want to have their baby taken care of at home. The baby usually gets more attention and there is less risk of infections. The most common situation is to have one of the parents stay home. Traditionally this has been the mother, but stay-at-home fathers are becoming common. Often the parent is making a permanent change in her or his career, but not always. Many parents return to work or their careers when their children are old enough to enter school.

It is estimated that over 1.5 million children are taken care of by someone other than a parent or relative. If you can afford it, you can hire a household employee or a nanny to take care of your baby at home.

If it's not possible to have one parent stay at home, it may be an option to have a friend or family member take care of the baby. Often this involves a grandparent. The advantage is that a relative is taking care of the baby, and you may not have to pay them. However, not every grandparent can or wants to take care of a baby, especially if they are advanced in age. Although many grandparents are sympathetic to the difficulties of finding good childcare, they often feel that they have already put in their time raising kids. They would rather spoil their grandchildren instead of taking care of them all day long.

Hiring a Nanny

Let's say you've decided to hire a nanny. How do you go about it, and what do you need to know? First, you can do some background homework before the baby is born, but you shouldn't consider interviewing until a few weeks before you need the nanny; most nannies are unlikely to wait for an extended period of time.

Finding a nanny can be very difficult. You might consider placing an ad in the paper, posting a flyer at your church, or asking other people with a nanny. Often you will have to go through an agency. The agency will send you a list of candidates whom they have screened through criminal background checks and references. If you select one of their choices, you will be expected to pay a certain amount for a finder's fee. This typically is about one month's salary. The applicant may also have to pay a certain amount of money.

> **Save yourself a lot of time and effort by calling up a prospective nanny's references. Be sure to ask about any gaps in her employment history.**

Interviewing

Interviewing a potential nanny is a key part of the hiring process. You and mom both have to be comfortable with the person you are going to hire. Have all your questions written down beforehand. You should conduct a phone interview before conducting one in person. If anything seems wrong, move on to another candidate. If you do offer her an interview, be sure to schedule enough time to see her interact with your baby. This includes playing, feeding, and diaper changing.

Salary

Salary is usually discussed in terms of dollars per week. Before deciding how much to offer, be sure to ask around to find out the going rate. Keep in mind that as the employer, you will be responsible for collecting state withholding and payroll taxes for Social Security and Medicare, which are an additional 15%. It is not uncommon to be competing against people who will be paying their nannies under the table. This means that you may end up having to pay 25% more than most others to make it legal.

Once a month or once a quarter you will have to pay the state her withholdings as well as unemployment insurance. You are not required to send in the payroll taxes or her federal withholding until you do your yearly taxes. Until then, it can stay in your accounts.

Benefits and Vacation

Most people who hire a nanny are not in a position to offer benefits, including health insurance or retirement. Other than you paying for unemployment insurance with the state and payroll taxes to qualify for Social Security, the nanny is usually on her own in terms of securing benefits.

Vacation time is highly negotiable and is often two weeks a year. Many parents insist from the beginning that the nanny's vacation correspond with their vacations, whereas others let the nanny choose far enough in advance to allow them to make arrangements. Be sure to cover this carefully before you make a job offer. It's important to have similar expectations from the very beginning.

Live-in Help

Some people with extra room in their house offer a nanny room and board in exchange for a reduced salary. The benefit is lower cost and increased flexibility. This is especially helpful if you or mom have irregular schedules, but it comes at the cost of privacy. The process for selecting a live-in nanny is the same, except you may want to pay particular attention to her housing history and why she is interested in being live-in help. If you are interested in a foreign live-in nanny (au pair), you will have to go through a special service authorized to arrange it.

Childcare Centers

Many couples don't have a relative who is capable or willing to take care of a baby at home, and most can't afford to hire a nanny either. As a result, they have to consider childcare centers. It can be a dramatic decision because of the guilt associated with "abandoning" your baby to strangers and exposing him to countless germs. The decision is especially difficult when the child is young and you can't justify it on the ground of socialization. Although it is substantially less expensive and generally more reliable than in-home care, the center may not be very flexible when it comes to irregular schedules. Also, most daycares are not equipped to handle sick children. This means that if your baby develops a fever, you will probably be asked to come pick up your child and keep him at home until he's well.

If you are considering placing your baby in daycare, be sure to check it out before the baby is born. In addition to getting a tour of the facility and meeting all the staff, you should observe some of the classes and get a number of references. Also, be sure to visit as many childcare centers in the area as you can.

For-Profit Daycare Centers

In response to increasing demand for childcare, many companies have stepped in to fill the void. They run the gamut from small mom-and-pop daycares to large national corporations. Since commercial daycares are regulated and licensed by your state, you can expect certain minimum requirements to be met, including child-to-adult ratios and building safety. However, compliance with these requirements and the quality of the individual attention or care can vary widely.

Not-for-Profit Daycare

A number of not-for-profit organizations, such as local churches, universities, and community outreach programs, are recognizing the need for low-cost quality daycare. These types of daycare centers tend to be better about offering financial aid or reducing fees to meet the needs of families, but they aren't as widely available as for-profit daycare centers.

Employer Daycare

An increasing number of progressive companies are recognizing the serious problem of getting good childcare and are developing on-site daycare for their employees. For employees, this usually means good childcare, close proximity, and supervision. This also allows for visits during the day and decreased guilt, and it generally costs less. For the employers, it can help attract and maintain top employees, and it may even have certain tax advantages. Unfortunately, because of their popularity, there is often a long waiting list to get in.

10

Planning for the Future

Being a parent means recognizing that you are responsible for the care and welfare of another person. An important part of being a new parent is recognizing that you will have financial responsibility for the baby for decades, if not longer. If you haven't spent time thinking about protecting yourself against financial catastrophe or planning for the future, now is the time to do so.

Insurance

When you are young, healthy, and relatively inexperienced, it is easy to underappreciate the importance of having good insurance. Many people assume nothing bad will happen, or that if something does, their parents will rescue them. Even when people do have insurance, they don't really understand the details and will often go for the cheapest options. All too often, when something does happen, they are not covered as they thought they were, and it can place severe financial hardship on a family. As an expectant father, review your insurance policies very carefully, and make sure your family will be adequately protected.

Health Insurance

Having a baby requires a lot of medical care. Even with an uncomplicated pregnancy, there will be bills for many office visits, lab tests, a hospitalization, and perhaps even major surgery. After the baby is born, you can expect even more lab tests, vaccinations (which may or may not be covered), and numerous visits to the pediatrician. So it is very important that you become very familiar with the details of your health insurance.

In-Network

In-network means that the health care provider has a contract with the insurance company to provide services for a set price. If you see someone outside of your network, you can expect to pay more (sometimes substantially more).

The term *health care provider* usually refers to such doctors as your obstetrician, anesthesiologist, and pediatrician—but not always. Many assistants, including nurse practitioners and physician assistants, are also able to bill directly.

Deductibles

A *deductible* is the amount of money that you have to pay before the insurance coverage begins. Until your deductible is met, you will be paying 100% of the costs. Typical deductibles range from $250 to $500 per person per year.

Co-Pays

Many insurance plans require that you pay a percentage of the bill up to a certain point. Typically this means after the deductible is met, you will be paying 20% of the bills until the cap is met.

Life Insurance

Health insurance is a critical part of developing a safety net for your family, but it is not enough. If your family is relying on your income, what happens if you die? For many people, Social Security benefits do not cover the expenses of a young family. Many companies provide a minimal amount of life insurance, but that is usually not enough. If your coverage is inadequate, you are going to have to purchase your own.

Amount of Life Insurance

The amount of life insurance you should carry depends on a number of factors. You should consider whether or not your partner is able to generate an income, your cost of living, the amount of Social Security your spouse would receive, how much debt you have, and what kind of assets you have. A general rule of thumb is to have insurance that is three times your household's gross yearly salary, which includes the amount of insurance you receive from your work.

Types of Life Insurance

There are many different kinds of life insurance policies, including term, whole life, universal life, and variable life. If you're looking for basic catastrophic coverage, term life insurance is the way to go. The premiums are the lowest, and they are fixed for a certain amount of time. If you are looking to use life insurance as a form of invest-

You cannot overestimate the importance of having enough life insurance now that you are expecting. Even though the odds are that your family will never need it, the security that it provides will protect them just in case, and it will definitely help you sleep better at night.

ment or for tax planning, you should talk to a financial adviser or insurance agent about your specific goals. For the vast majority of new parents, term life insurance is the clear choice.

Duration

Assuming that you are interested in term insurance, you typically have a choice of 10, 15, 20, and 30 years. This means that during this time period, your premium should stay the same, and you can't be canceled. After that, you may be able to continue the policy, but you can expect the premiums to rise dramatically. In most cases, a 20-year policy will protect your family until your children are old enough for college. In the meantime, you should be saving and accumulating assets.

Costs

The amount you pay depends not only on the type and duration of the insurance but also on your health. If you are young and healthy and have no preexisting medical conditions, you should be eligible for the best rates or the lowest premiums. Make sure there are no commissions, hidden charges, or other penalties when purchasing a policy.

> If you smoke or have a chronic illness, such as diabetes, you aren't going to qualify for the low rates that insurance companies like to advertise. You represent a higher risk to them, and they are going to charge you accordingly.

Disability Insurance

Health insurance and life insurance offer some security, but they are not enough. What happens if you are injured and unable to work? It is more likely that someone young will become disabled rather than die. This is why disability insurance is much more expensive, costing as much as 2–3% of your income. Because of a wide variety of available options, getting disability insurance is much more complicated than getting life insurance. Depending on your age and health risks, you may not be able to get an individual policy. If this is the case, your only option is to get a group policy offered through a company or other organization. In general, these types of policies don't inquire about individual medical histories or require a physical examination.

Types of Disability Insurance

There are two types of disability policies: short-term disability (STD) and long-term disability (LTD). Short-term disability is intended to cover a condition that is expected to last for less than two years. Long-term disability is for disabilities that are career ending.

Waiting Period

Most policies have a waiting period between when you are declared disabled and when you are paid. For STD, it can be a matter of days, whereas LTD can take weeks to months. The longer the waiting period, the lower the premiums.

Benefit Amount

The amount you can expect to receive if you are disabled is usually expressed as a monthly payment. In almost all cases, the amount will be substantially lower than your current or potential income. This is because the insurance company doesn't want to give you an incentive not to work. Also, the insurance company usually sets a maximum amount you can receive by coordinating the benefits from all your policies, including Social Security. It is very difficult to get a disability policy with benefits of more than $10,000 per month.

Because many employers use short-term disability policies to pay for maternity leave, your partner might be eligible for paid maternity leave. If so, it is very important for mom to talk to the human resources person at her company as soon as she makes her pregnancy public.

Taxes

If your employer pays for the policy, any money you receive while disabled will be considered income and reported to the IRS. This typically happens if you are covered under a company's group policy. If you have an individual policy that, whether as a primary or secondary, you pay for with post-tax dollars, the payments are not taxable.

Type of Work

Some disabilities are more debilitating than others. An increasing number of policies are being written such that they won't pay if you can do any work, not just your current job. This makes it very important that you get a policy that covers you specifically if you are not able to perform your particular type of work.

Cost of Living Adjustments (COLA)

For a higher premium, you can have the disability benefits increase over time to cover cost of living increases. This type of option is usually tied to the consumer price index (CPI). Without this option, a fixed benefit would have less and less purchasing power over time. If you are permanently disabled, this can be significant 10–20 years down the line.

Termination

Most group disability policies obtained through work are usually canceled if you leave your company. This means that if you develop a medical condition while you're unemployed, you may not be able to get coverage unless you are part of another group policy. For this reason, it is often a good idea to get an individual policy that can't be terminated except for lack of payment.

Homeowners Insurance

Homeowners insurance is usually required when you obtain a mortgage to buy a home. Banks and mortgage brokers require a certain minimum to protect their investment, but it doesn't cover everything. It is important that you meet with your insurance agent to make sure you understand your policy in detail, and to make changes if necessary. It is particularly important to know what is included, what is excluded, what are the deductibles, and whether they pay cash value or replacement costs. You should also inquire about premium reductions by getting a home alert system.

Insurance Against Property Damage

Property damage insurance typically protects the house against fire, explosion, lightning, windstorm or hail, theft, and vandalism. A certain amount of personal property is covered, excluding jewelry and other valuables. Most policies typically exclude earthquakes, landslide, flood, tidal waves, sewer backup, nuclear radiation, terrorism, and war.

Liability Coverage

Almost all policies protect you and your family in the event that someone sues you claiming negligence due to an injury or damage to their property. The insurance will cover the defense costs regardless of the outcome. If you are found liable, they will pay for damages up to a certain limit. Anything over the limit is your responsibility.

Medical Payments

Some coverage is provided for accidental injury to others when it occurs on your

If your home is severely damaged by something excluded from your policy, you are still responsible for the mortgage, even if you can't rebuild or live in the house. As a young parent, you probably won't have the resources to pay for the rebuilding yourself, and you might have to declare bankruptcy.

property, whether you are responsible or not. With today's high health costs, it isn't much. It also does not cover you or members of your family.

Damage to Property of Others

A policy typically covers up to $500 worth of minor damage that is accidentally caused by someone in your family.

Loss of Use

Loss of use covers the increase in living expenses that becomes necessary if the house cannot be occupied due to something covered by the policy (e.g., a fire).

Car Insurance

If you own a car, having good insurance is important for protecting your assets. Although car insurance can be expensive, the cost of an uninsured accident where you are liable, especially if there is an injury, can bankrupt your family. Even if you think your car insurance is adequate, you need to review it just to be sure. For many people, the coverage turns out to be less than they thought, and they purchase supplemental insurance. Also, there are a number of options for deductibles. The higher the deductible, the more you have to pay before the insurance begins coverage, but the premium is lower.

Saving for College

College costs are very high and are increasing faster than inflation. According to the College Board, for tuition and fees, the average 4-year public college costs $5,836, and the average 4-year private college is $22, 218 for the 2006–07 school year. Assuming that the cost of college is increasing 7% per year, and your baby goes to college in 18 years, you will have to save roughly $77,000 to send him to public school or $300,000 to send him to private school. This doesn't even include room and board!

So whether you have the extra money or not to save for college at this moment, now is still a good time to start learning about the options.

Unlike funding your retirement, there is currently no way to save for college and get a tax deduction. The best you can hope for is to avoid paying the taxes on the earnings from investing for college. However, this isn't always possible, especially if you are a high-income earner.

529 College Saving Plans

The 529 college saving plan is considered by many to be the best way to save for college. The main advantages are that the earnings in 529 plans grow entirely tax free, and many states are even offering tax deductions for the contributions. You, or anyone else for that matter, can contribute to a 529 regardless of your level of income. Although there is a limit on the amount of money that can be invested, it is very substantial at $300,000 per beneficiary. The downside is that there are numerous 529 plans to choose from, and there can be substantial fees, including front- and/or back-end sales fees. It is important to realize that the benefits of a tax-deferred or tax-exempt plan can be eroded quickly

Even if you don't have the money to fund a 529 plan right now, you should still consider setting one up when the baby is born. Many grandparents like the idea of partially funding their grandchildren's education with gifts or as part of their estate planning.

during a bear market, especially when there are high fees. Even if you qualify for a state deduction, it may not make up the difference.

Uniform Gifts to Minors Act/Uniform Transfers to Minors Act (UGMA/UTMA)

Before 529 plans came along, UGMA or UTMA accounts were the preferred method of saving for college or transferring wealth. Although the accounts were set up in the child's name, the "custodian" of the account was responsible for its management. The first $850 in earnings is free from federal taxes and the next $850 is taxed at the child's tax rate, which is normally lower than that of an adult. The downside to these accounts is that after $1,700, the earnings are taxed at the custodian's tax rate, and the child can assume control once he is 18 years old for UGMA or 21 for UTMA.

Coverdell Education Savings Accounts (ESA)

Education savings accounts used to be known as the Education IRA. Unlike other plans, this one lets you save for any level of education, including elementary school. With ESAs, there is tax-deferred growth, and the earnings are tax-free if used for qualified educational expenses. As of 2004, they are not considered parent or student income, and thus do not reduce one's eligibility for financial aid. There is a limit of $2,000 per year, regardless of the number of contributors to the account. Although in theory you can contribute to both an ESA and a 529 plan, you may not qualify for the ESA if your income is too high.

Savings Bonds

Buying U.S. savings bonds is one of the safest ways to save for college. Not only are they backed by the full faith and credit of the U.S. government, the interest may be tax deferrable and possibly tax exempt. Generally you won't have to pay state or local income tax on the interest they earn. The federal tax is deferred until the bonds are redeemed. If you use the bonds to pay for college, the interest could be tax exempt, depending on your income level. There are two types of U.S. savings bonds to consider: the Series I and the Series EE bonds. The Series I bond can protect you from inflation because it is based on the Consumer Price Index for all urban consumers (the CPI-U). The Series EE bond is a fixed-rate bond that is tied to the 10-year Treasury average. You have to be 24 years old to buy them, and there is a per-person limit of $15,000 for Series EE bonds and $30,000 for Series I bonds.

Saving for Retirement

Before the baby came along, you might not have thought much about saving for retirement. You might even be tempted to forgo saving for retirement if you are relatively young and in desperate need of the money. However, this may be a mistake. By putting money away early and in tax-preferred vehicles, you increase the chances that you will be better prepared for retirement when your baby is ready to start college. This is especially true if your employer has a matching program to which they contribute based on how much you set aside. Also, at the present time, assets in retirement accounts are not held against students in determining financial aid. This isn't true for all educational vehicles. Another consideration is that certain types of retirement plans allow you to pull out contributions or borrow against the account for educational expenses. Ironically, by not having to worry about playing catch-up with your retirement savings, you will be in a better position to help pay for college if the college savings fall short. Therefore, maximize your retirement savings as much as possible. There are several traditional retirement programs for employees as well as the self-employed or small-business owner.

Employer-Sponsored Plans

The easiest and most popular way to save for retirement is by having your company do it for you.

Providing for your own retirement is an important part of planning ahead for your child. The last thing you want is for your baby to be struggling to support both you and his own family in 30 or 40 years.

Pensions

Until recently, contributing to a pension plan was the most common way to save for retirement. These plans are usually offered by large corporations and government agencies. The risk of pension plans being underfunded or susceptible to elimination in bankruptcy is increasing. In theory, the government may insure some of them, but in reality, they are not completely secure. Companies are increasingly shifting from pensions to other retirement vehicles.

401(k) Plans

The 401(k) is currently the most popular employer-offered plan. It lets you invest a portion of your salary in a tax-deferred vehicle. This means that the amount you contribute is subtracted from your taxable income and the return on your investment isn't taxed until you withdraw the money, usually after the age of 59½. As a bonus, many companies will match your contribution up to a certain point. However, the amount you can contribute is limited and changes on a yearly basis, and you must use the investment vehicles chosen by your company.

It is increasingly common for large companies coming out of bankruptcy to limit their health care and pension obligations to their retirees. This makes relying solely on your company's pension risky, because there is no guarantee that your company won't also face some catastrophic turn of events in the future.

403(b) Plans

A 403(b) plan is similar to a 401(k) plan except that it is for non-profit organizations. Contributions are limited to 20% of your salary or $15,000 (whichever is less). They are exempt from state and federal taxes, and earnings are tax deferred. Contribution limits are increased for older employers (age 50 or older) and those with 15 or more years of experience. Similar to 401(k) plans, there is a yearly increase to cover the cost of living.

Individual Retirement Accounts (IRAs)

Anyone who has an income that comes from being employed can contribute to an IRA. Whether or not you get a tax deduction for it depends on the type of IRA and your income level. There are several types of IRAs available, and you should consider each carefully to see what works best for you and your family.

Traditional IRA

The traditional IRA is an option for tax-advantaged growth on earnings that is set up individually (not sponsored by your employer). It can be set up through any number of financial institutions. Contributions are lower and are limited by the amount of income earned or $4,000 (whichever is less). Your contributions may or may not be deductible, depending on your income level. It is also possible to set one up for mom, even if she isn't working or generating much income.

Roth IRA

The Roth IRA is an individual option for tax-advantaged growth on earnings. Your contributions are made in post-tax dollars; therefore, it offers no tax deductions. This means you can withdraw the contributions, but not the earnings, at any time without penalty or tax. Contributions are lower and are limited by the amount of income earned or $4,000, whichever is less. Unlike other retirement vehicles, it is available only to those who earn

Self-employment retirement plans often allow you to contribute more than most employers' plans, and thus allow for greater tax savings. However, there are also restrictions. For example, if you have employees, you may be required to provide coverage for them that is comparable to your own.

below a certain amount—$95,000 for single filers and $150,000 for joint filers for 2006.

Self-Employed Plans

Many self-employed or small-business owners may think more about growing their business than about how to set up a retirement plan. Although it does take some additional work, it is worth the benefits.

SEP-IRA

The SEP-IRA (Simplified Employee Pension IRA) is a retirement plan that is specifically designed for self-employed people and small-business owners. It is easy to set up and maintain with flexible funding requirements. The contributions are tax deductible but limited to 25% of your compensation, with a maximum of $44,000. The contribution limit has recently increased, making the SEP-IRA competitive with the Keogh plan.

Keogh Plans

Before the changes to the SEP-IRA, Keogh plans allowed for higher contributions. Despite their increased paperwork requirements, they are often still used because they allow the business owner more options in setting up a plan. For example, using various vesting schedules and profit-sharing options, the business owner or owners can legally fund their retirement accounts better, relative to those of their employees.

Estate Planning

Contrary to what the name suggests, you don't need to be rich and have an estate to benefit from estate planning. In fact, you don't actually need an attorney to handle it. There are a number of software programs that will help you generate basic legal documents that are valid in your state. The key is to make sure you have the document properly witnessed. However, if you have sizable assets or you suspect that it might get contested in court by one of your family members, then paying for an attorney is probably worth it.

Wills

A will is a set of instructions on how to take care of and distribute your possessions. If you die without one, the state government will decide what happens to your assets. There is no guarantee that your family or friends will inherit anything. Also, once your baby is born, it will be very important for you and mom to declare the person (or persons) that you want to take care of your baby if something should happen to you both. If a guardian isn't named, then the state will decide for you through the courts and social service agencies.

Living Wills

A living will is an extension of your basic will with the difference being that you are still alive. It is principally used to tell doctors, hospitals, and anyone else what your wishes for medical care are. For example, it lets people know whether you would want to refuse life-support measures under futile conditions. In

As an expectant father, you need to realize that if you are severely injured and in a permanent coma, your life insurance won't pay out.

the absence of a living will, your doctors will have to assume you want everything reasonable to be done to keep you alive.

Medical Power of Attorney

If you prefer not to spell out exactly what your wishes are, but would rather have someone such as mom make the decisions based on the specific situation, then a medical power of attorney is for you. It gives whomever you want the legal authority to make medical decisions on your behalf. This is usually more appropriate for younger people.

Part Three

Taking It One Month at a Time

11

Month 1

The first month of pregnancy is calculated as starting at the end of mom's last menstrual period and ending after week 4. This might seem a little confusing—that mom isn't actually pregnant during the "first two weeks" of the pregnancy. But there is a reason for this method of calculation. It is usually easier to remember the first day of her last menstrual period than the date conception likely occurred, so this calculation leads to a more accurate estimation of the baby's due date.

What's Happening with the Baby

Shortly after mom's egg is released from one of her ovaries, your sperm will meet up with it in her Fallopian tube. After one of the millions of sperm you released has successfully made it inside the egg, a protective shield will form around it, and all the other sperm will be kept out. The fertilized egg will then start to divide, and a number of new and identical cells will be created. While all this is happening, this ball of cells will be making its way to its new home in the uterus.

What May Be Happening with Her

Unless you and mom are actively trying to get pregnant, the first month will probably be over before she realizes she is pregnant. However, if mom is trying to get pregnant, she may be very determined to try to have sex around the time she is ovulating. Because of the relatively narrow window of time when your sperm has the chance to fertilize her released egg, she may become very anxious. She may even track her body temperature or check the hormone levels in her urine to find out when she is about to ovulate.

> Sometimes the egg gets stuck in the Fallopian tube. This is called an ectopic, or tubal, pregnancy. This type of pregnancy must be terminated to protect the life of the mother.

What You Can Expect

You have no doubt heard that pregnant women can be very emotional. What you might not realize is that expectant fathers experience new emotions, too. Because men often don't like to talk about our feelings, it is easy to assume that we are the only ones experiencing them. As an expectant father, recognizing your emotions (both positive and negative) is an important part of the pregnancy.

> You should not be concerned if you don't experience every single emotion, or if the timing of your emotions is different from what other men experience. No two expectant fathers are the same.

Realizing That Your Life Is about to Change

If this is your first pregnancy, this is going to be one of the most exciting periods of your life. You may have already begun to realize that you and mom are going to be experiencing a lot of changes in your lives. Having a baby inevitably means that one phase of your life is over and another has started.

Fears of Losing Your Independence

Having a family that depends on you means you won't always be able to do what you want, when you want. Faced with this change, many expectant fathers at one time or another experience the feeling of being trapped. Eventually you will realize that the richness that having children brings to your life can only happen when you let go of your independence.

Feelings of Uncertainty and Doubt

Having a baby is a big decision. It is right up there with getting married, buying your first house, and starting a new career or your own business. Any time you take a big risk there is a chance that you are going to have some uncertainty or doubt. You may wonder whether it is a good idea, whether the timing is right, or any number of other questions.

> **These feelings will likely come and go during the pregnancy, but as soon as you hold your new baby, your doubts will disappear and you will know it was the right decision.**

Feelings of Anxiety

Having a baby on the way is going to dramatically increase your responsibilities, not only to your unborn child but to mom as well. It is only natural that you will worry about the future and how it is going to affect your family. You will suddenly realize that you have more to lose. You may feel that you cannot control everything affecting your family, and that bad things can happen. This will invoke anxiety and worry. This is actually a good thing. It will give you the energy, motivation, and ability to concentrate and focus on the things you need to address to provide for and protect your family. Fear is one of life's best motivators, but you must be careful not to let it get out of control and become irrational. If you can't seem to shake the anxiety or you begin to perseverate, you need to step back reevaluate the situation.

What's Going on with Prenatal Care

To help improve the odds that mom has an uneventful pregnancy and a healthy baby, she should take some basic precautions one to two months before trying to get pregnant. Two of the most important precautions are taking prenatal vitamins and avoiding alcohol. By taking prenatal vitamins, not only will she be helping to prevent birth defects in the baby, she will also be preventing deficiencies of important minerals such as calcium and iron during the pregnancy. By avoiding alcohol, whether in the form of an occasional drink or binge drinking, she will be preventing development of a condition called fetal alcohol syndrome. This is where the baby is born small, usually with some mental retardation, and a number of deformities involving the head, heart, and limbs.

What You Two Should Be Discussing

To give your baby the best possible chance of being born without a birth defect, mom will need to do a number of additional things starting around the time the baby is conceived. By working together, you can make it easier for her and help her be more successful.

Avoiding Tobacco and Recreational Drugs

There is no question that smoking and taking recreational drugs can be harmful during pregnancy. Almost everyone recognizes that it is safest to avoid smoking and taking drugs during pregnancy. Unfortunately, tobacco and drugs can be physically and emotionally addictive, and they are therefore very hard to stop. Stopping your own use and going with mom to consult a cessation counselor may be the first steps to helping her quit.

Good Diet and Nutrition

It is getting harder and harder to eat nutritiously in our fast-paced society. Gaining weight from eating too much "junk food" is not healthy for mom or the baby. Also, she should avoid foods that may be harmful to the baby, such as caffeinated beverages and undercooked meat. The sooner you and mom start thinking about how to plan healthy meals and determine what foods she should avoid, the better.

Exercise

Many women think of exercise only in terms of weight loss. However, it can be very important in helping mom's body meet the increased demands of the pregnancy and can help her tolerate the normal discomfort of weight gain. Working with mom from the beginning to develop a consistent, safe exercise routine will make it more likely she will stick with it throughout the pregnancy.

Medications

All medications, including over-the-counter drugs, have the potential of causing birth defects. Ideally, mom's doctor will check them out individually. If this hasn't been done, it is be a good idea to research their safety on the Internet. To help assess the risk, the U.S. Food and Drug Administration (FDA) has developed a rating system. If any of mom's medications poses a risk or has not been tested for safety during pregnancy, she should discuss this during her first doctor's visit.

Supplements and Herbs

Despite widespread misconceptions, the fact that something is natural does not necessarily mean it is safe, especially during a pregnancy. Supplements and herbs are not regulated by the FDA and are not rated for safety. As a result, their use should be discontinued and be avoided unless specifically approved by a doctor. Depending on mom's beliefs, it may take some effort to convince her of their potential dangers.

What You Should Be Asking Yourself

The expectant father has two main obligations when a baby is on the way. The first is to do everything he can to help his partner through the pregnancy process. The second is to do everything he can to make sure he is ready to be a father. In order to do both, you need to be proactive and to constantly question yourself.

> You don't need special training in counseling or psychotherapy to help with mom's anxiety. Research has repeatedly shown that for most people, talking to someone who cares will cause them to feel better, even if nothing is resolved.

Am I Ready to Be There for Her?

Being pregnant can be an exciting and joyful time in a woman's life, but it is not without a reasonable amount of anxiety. Anxiety is a normal response to stress, and there is no doubt that having a baby is stressful. Although anxiety helps you cope by making you focused on the particular issue at hand, if no action is taken in response to the stress, and if issues are not resolved, the anxiety can become excessive and even irrational. In other words, if mom holds on to and internalizes her worries, she will exacerbate them and make them "larger than life." You need to let her express her opinions, concerns, and beliefs. Are you ready to suspend judgment and refrain from attempting to direct her to your own points of view?

Am I Ready to Think about Changes?

Being a good father will likely mean that you have to make changes in your priorities and in your relationships with your friends, family, and coworkers. Many expectant fathers don't want to take the time to anticipate and work out these issues in advance. Instead, they are more comfortable ignoring them and hoping matters will all work out later. Unfortunately, this can lead to unresolved issues that can suddenly explode during a period of stress. Are you ready to take the time to anticipate how the baby is going to affect your life?

Thinking about this now is particularly important if you already have a complicated, busy, or demanding life. (What do you think is going to happen when the baby is born?) Unless you are prepared to deal with the constant stress of trying to balance your old life with your new life, you need to be willing to make some changes. You need to accept that your new family is your highest priority and that it may require you to give up parts of your old life.

What You Should Be Doing

Pregnancy is a time of anticipation and preparation. Most of the preparations for the baby traditionally have been taken care of by the expectant mother, but not anymore. As an expectant father you should be doing everything you can to help and take stress off of mom.

Understand Your Health Insurance

Having a baby requires a great deal of prenatal and medical care. Being familiar with your health insurance is important in selecting a health care provider or hospital. Knowing the terms of your insurance policy will help you to estimate what your out-of-pocket expenses will be.

Help Her Organize Her Medical History

Mom's doctor will need to know her complete medical history. Having all of her medical information and health records available and organized before the first doctor's visit will help ensure that mom and baby get the best possible prenatal care.

Look for Illnesses That Run in Your Family

Many birth defects are caused by disorders that run in the father's or the mother's family. By learning more about your family history, you may discover that your baby is at risk for a disease that can be diagnosed with genetic testing.

Show Her You Are Excited about Being a Father

Having a baby can lead to many changes and fears in an expectant mother, as well as in the expectant father. Expressing excitement—even if you don't feel it at this particular moment—can go a long way toward reassuring her that she will not be going through it alone.

12

Month 2

The second month of pregnancy starts with week 5 and ends after week 8. It is the middle of the first trimester, and for many women it is the month when they first suspect and then confirm that they are pregnant. It is an important period in your baby's development and in mom's prenatal medical care. It may also be the beginning of the next phase of your life.

What's Happening with the Baby

By now, the baby is firmly established in the uterus and a critical phase of development has begun. All the major body organs are starting to form and the baby's heart has started to beat. The head, arms, and legs have developed to the point that the baby is no longer called an embryo, but a fetus. Despite this, by the end of the month, the baby still weighs only a fraction of an ounce and is without a functioning placenta.

What May Be Happening with Her

Although the baby is still very tiny, he will be starting to have a big impact on mom's body. The release of a large amount of female hormones leads to the characteristic symptoms of pregnancy. Women who haven't been pregnant before may not immediately recognize them as signs of pregnancy. Those who have, however, often know right away. Once your partner suspects that she may be pregnant, she will likely confirm it with a home urine pregnancy test.

> **Home pregnancy tests are very accurate and can detect pregnancy as early as ten days after fertilization. If the result of the pregnancy test is positive, there is no need to repeat the test, and mom should call her doctor. Even if the test result is negative, there is a chance mom may be pregnant, and she should wait a couple of days before testing again.**

Morning Sickness

Nausea and vomiting are very common early in pregnancy. For most women, these symptoms are relatively mild, but for some, they can be severe. Even though it is called "morning sickness," it can happen any time of the day. If mom has problems with morning sickness, you might suggest that she eat frequent but small meals to avoid an empty stomach, drink enough fluids (typically eight 8-ounce glasses of water), and avoid pungent smells and fatty or hard-to-digest foods. If mom is having a hard time keeping anything down, has dark concentrated urine or urinates infrequently, and is not gaining or losing weight, she should call her doctor.

Breast Changes

Almost from the beginning of the pregnancy, the increased amounts of female hormones will likely cause mom to have breast tingling, swelling, or tenderness. Later, mom's breasts are going to increase in size, often dramatically, as the milk glands enlarge and fat builds up in preparation for breastfeeding.

Fatigue

Most women experience fatigue during pregnancy, usually during the first and third trimesters. Early on, production of progesterone, a key pregnancy hormone, can make mom feel very tired and sleepy. This usually improves during the second trimester. During the third trimester, when she is very large, uncomfortable, and not sleeping well, the fatigue can return.

To help with the fatigue, you should encourage mom to get plenty of rest, drink enough fluids (at least 1–2 liters of water a day), take adequate iron (at least a 30 mg supplement), avoid stressful situations, and exercise if it is not against doctor's orders.

> **Take on additional responsibilities and chores so that she doesn't overexert herself or so that she can take an extra nap. If she is stressing out about something, see if you can help her talk it out or run interference for her.**

Frequent Urination

Many women start to urinate more frequently after becoming pregnant. Other than being a little annoying, it is not a problem unless it is a sign of uncontrolled diabetes (usually indicated by a lot of urine) or a urinary tract infection.

What You Can Expect

The difference between trying to have a baby and actually having a baby on the way is huge. So it is not surprising if you experience a dramatic change in feelings practically overnight.

Excitement and Amazement

When you found out that you were going to be a father you were probably very excited. When you realized that two tiny little cells will be developing into a baby in as little as nine months, you were probably amazed as well. During the pregnancy and throughout your life as a father, there are going to be quite a few times when you will have these moments. Unfortunately, they can't last all the time. It is a fact of nature that it is impossible to be excited all the time. We

Depending on the circumstances, you may not have been utterly thrilled when you first heard that mom was pregnant. If you haven't yet allowed yourself to feel excited or amazed, don't worry. It will happen.

tend to reset our emotions to a certain baseline after a relatively short period of time. So, when you do experience them, you should really savor them.

Feelings of Pride

At one point or another, you are going to feel proud about becoming a father. What causes these feelings depends on what is important to you, but very likely it will have to do with being associated with something as wonderful as a baby. In fact, some of your most intense moments of pride will occur when the baby's presence seems most real—for example, when you see him on the ultrasound monitor, when you hear his heartbeat, when you feel him kicking, and especially when you hold him for the first time.

Realizing You Are Going to Have Your Own Family

When you were growing up, you might have been in a close-knit family. But being in a family is not the same as having your own family. Before you were expecting a baby, you might have thought that you and your partner were a family. Having your lives seem completely inseparable—so that you couldn't imagine your life without her—is certainly a good start, but it's not enough. Now that you are expecting a baby, you are probably starting to realize that you are going to be part of something bigger than the two of you. When your baby is finally born, you will fully realize that you are part of something truly special—something that did not exist the day before.

What's Going on with Prenatal Care

During the initial visit to the doctor, mom will undergo an extensive evaluation, including a comprehensive medical history and physical examination, as well as a battery of blood, urine, and other prenatal tests. Most of the tests are standard for every pregnancy.

Medical History

Unless mom has had the same doctor for a long time, the doctor will spend some time learning mom's gynecological, obstetrical, and medical history. Having all the information available (including previous pertinent medical records) can speed up this process a lot.

Physical Examination

After taking a complete history, the doctor will examine mom for signs of unrecognized illnesses. Particularly important are high blood pressure and heart problems such as valvular disease. She will also undergo a pelvic exam if one has not recently been done.

Initial Tests

The doctor will order a number of blood and urine tests to check mom's blood type and counts, and will screen for infections and illnesses known to complicate pregnancy. The results will be available at the next prenatal visit.

Estimating a Due Date

Based on mom's menstrual history, and possibly on findings from a vaginal ultrasound, the doctor will estimate a due date for the baby. Realize that this is only an estimation, and that the baby may arrive anywhere from two weeks before to two weeks after the estimated due date.

What You Two Should Be Discussing

Finding out that your partner is pregnant can be very exciting, especially if you have been trying for a while. But not everyone realizes that a large percentage of pregnancies terminate in miscarriage within the first trimester. In many ways, this is a good thing. Genetic shuffling of chromosomes doesn't always turn out the way it should. Miscarriage is the body's way of rejecting a failed attempt at combining two different sets of genes.

Telling Family and Friends

By the end of week 13, or the first trimester, your doctor should be able to verify that the baby is in the preferred position and has a good heartbeat. When this is the case, the chances of a successful pregnancy rise dramatically. If you have to tell someone earlier, it is a good idea to tell only family or very close friends. Also, it is a very good idea to be cautious. Emphasize how early it is, but that you are excited and hoping for the best.

Telling People at Work

Telling people at work may be a little trickier. You understandably want to tell the people you spend so much of your time with, but you need to consider that a baby is going to have an effect on your job and on your relationship with others. Many people will be genuinely happy for you but they will also be evaluating how the new baby will affect them. Make sure you have thought things through before announcing your good news.

Telling Your Children

When you tell your other children depends on how old and mature they are. It is certainly prudent to wait at least until the second trimester, in case a problem with the pregnancy should arise. However, you don't want to wait too long because you want them to feel included and not threatened by their new sibling.

> **If mom has a job that exposes her to radiation or other hazards to your baby, then she will have to tell her employer sooner than she may have preferred to. Because the baby's susceptibility to birth defects is highest during the first trimester, mom can't afford to wait.**

What You Should Be Asking Yourself

It is not uncommon for a newly pregnant woman to feel as though her symptoms are not being taken as seriously as they might be if she were eight months pregnant and "really showing." You should ask yourself whether mom is getting the sense that you are involved in the pregnancy.

Am I Making Her Life Easier?

During the pregnancy, mom will have times when it is hard for her to take care of errands and other tasks that she used to handle easily. This is especially true when she is suffering from fatigue or morning sickness in the beginning, and when she becomes huge toward the end. If you are part of a dual-worker family, you are probably splitting up the chores already. If not, it may be something of a change for you. Take care of errands such as shopping for groceries or cleaning the house. Run interference for her and help keep her from getting overextended. Set time aside for doing research about pregnancy.

> By anticipating and eliminating (or minimizing) sources of stress and frustration for mom, you will be making your life easier as well.

How Will I Be Involved during the Pregnancy?

Being involved during the pregnancy does more than just show mom that you care. It is also necessary for building a strong parental bond. The more time you spend, the stronger the bond and the more you will value it. Although you might think that there really isn't much for you to do during the pregnancy, there is. You need to spend time learning about the pregnancy, going to prenatal appointments when you can, and asking questions and getting answers to them. You need to communicate with mom about what is going on with her. You also need to participate in pregnancy decisions, even if mom seems to have already made up her mind.

> The more involved you are during the pregnancy, the more invested you become. As a result, you will be more interested in the pregnancy process.

What You Should Be Doing

Although this month marks a momentous event in your life, it is probably a bigger deal for mom. This is an important time to show her your enthusiasm about being an expectant father and the pregnancy.

Tell Her How Excited You Are

For a woman, being pregnant is one of the most special and important moments of life, especially if it is the first pregnancy. Even if mom has been talking about it for some time, the fact that it has now happened still makes it a very special moment. Letting her know that she is not alone in her excitement can really give this pregnancy a good start.

Try to Go to the First Doctor's Visit

Over the next nine months, you partner will likely have 15 or more prenatal doctor visits. It may not be practical for you to attend every one of them, but you should try to go to the first one. Not only will it allow you to show your support, but it will also give you a chance to meet the doctor who will likely be delivering your baby.

Help Her Cut Back on Unnecessary Commitments

If mom is one of those people who can't say no to anyone, or who tends to take on too many things at once, she may need your help to cut down on unnecessary commitments and prioritize her time. She will be going through a lot of emotional and physical changes over the next eight months, and she needs to be able to focus on preparations and on getting enough rest. It may be easier for you to run interference for her than for her to say no.

Help Take Care of Errands at Home

Over the next few months, mom is going to need you to help free up some of her time at home. By taking care of errands such as shopping for groceries or cleaning the house, you will give her a chance to take a nap, which is very important if she is having a lot of fatigue, or to read about the pregnancy. The more rested and prepared she is, the less stressful and anxious she will be.

Start Calling Her at Least Once a Day

Not only will a regular phone call demonstrate how important she and the baby are to you, it will also give her a chance to let you know what she is feeling. If something is bothering her, you want her to talk about it sooner rather than later.

13

Month 3

The third month of pregnancy starts with week 9 and ends after week 13. It is the end of the first trimester and a very anxious time for some pregnant women. Many of the initial test results will be back, and it's possible that not all of them will be normal. Also, until this month is over, there remains a reasonable chance that the pregnancy could end in a spontaneous miscarriage.

What's Happening with the Baby

By this point, the main body organs are all in place, the face is formed, and the brain and nervous system are developing nicely. The bone and muscles are being rapidly put in place, giving the baby some structure. The genital organs are still forming, so it is still too early to tell the baby's sex. By the end of this month, the baby will be almost fully formed, 3 inches long, and recognizably human.

What May Be Happening with Her

The pregnancy hormones are still surging, so mom is likely to be very tired and suffering from morning sickness. She is also likely to be very emotional, with moods swinging from ecstatic to sad and weepy. Her interest in sex may well drop off because of the force of surging hormones and because of not feeling well. You may start hearing mom talk about "eating for two," and express cravings for new or different types of foods. She may also suddenly find that something she used to like to eat now makes her sick to her stomach.

Moodiness

All the hormones, combined with the stress of pregnancy, can make pregnant women moody. One minute they can be on top of the world, and the next they'll be crying and very needy. It is best not to overreact to the moodiness, and just do what you can to help.

Decreased Libido

Being tired, having headaches, and experiencing decreased libido can be par for the course in early pregnancy. If mom is not particularly interested in sex at this time, do not take it as a personal rejection.

Headaches

Headaches are relatively common during pregnancy. No one knows for sure why they happen, but they are thought to be caused by hormones and changes in the blood vessels. Also, some women experience new or worsening tension headaches and migraines made more acute by stress, fatigue, lack of sleep, and caffeine withdrawal.

Food Cravings

Many pregnant women have food cravings, some very intense and others just plain strange. These are thought to be caused by hormonal and emotional changes. Be prepared to make trips to the grocery store for unexpected purchases.

Food Aversions

It isn't clear why a pregnant woman can have a sudden and very negative reaction to food that she otherwise may like. Some doctors believe the food aversion is triggered by some gastrointestinal defense mechanism that we don't understand. In any case, try to avoid eating foods that produce such a reaction in her presence.

What You Can Expect

Unless you are a seasoned veteran or someone with a lot of health care experience, all the prenatal care activity of the first trimester can make it a very intimidating time for an expectant father.

Feeling Ignorant

Unless you have been through a pregnancy before or have read a stack of books, you are going to feel as though you don't know a thing. Almost every guy feels ignorant during the entire first pregnancy. It's important not to be satisfied with your ignorance but to be motivated to overcome it. The best way to overcome ignorance is to recognize what you don't know, make a list of questions, and then get answers to your questions.

Feeling Not in Control

There is a tremendous amount of responsibility and many decisions to make when you are preparing for a baby. Many of these decisions are going to be made by mom and her doctor. Unless you spend as much time as mom learning about pregnancy, attend every prenatal visit, and take part in every decision, you are going to be out of the loop to a certain degree. You will likely not have a grasp of everything that is going on, and thus you cannot be in control. If things are going well, this probably won't be an issue. If things aren't going well, or if there is a big decision to make, you are going to feel helpless to a degree. To minimize these feelings, learn as much as you can and participate in decisions as much as possible.

Instincts to Protect Your New Family

After hearing of their pending fatherhood, most men experience an evolutionarily driven urge to protect their partner and their unborn child from danger. Although modern society offers defenses against many of the perils of the past—such as starvation, wild animals, catastrophic weather, and treatable infections—many dangers do remain. One of your primary roles as expectant father will be to protect mom and baby from these dangers.

Many people assume that because childbirth is natural, it must be safe. However, until recently, childbirth was a relatively common cause of death for young women, and many babies suffered complications at birth. Without good prenatal and obstetric care, childbirth cannot be considered completely safe for any mother or baby.

Some dangers are obvious (such as violent crime and accidents), but many are not. Not everyone realizes the prevalence of poisons, infections, and occupational hazards in the modern environment. Too few people realize that medications and herbs can hurt the baby, particularly during the first trimester. Although mom is going to be just as concerned as you (if not more), you can't defer all the responsibility to her. You must be just as attentive, and always on the lookout for potential danger.

Fearing That Something Might Go Wrong

It is extremely common for an expectant father to worry about the well-being of his partner and his baby. However, with good prenatal care and the medical advances available today, mom and your baby should be in good hands.

What's Going on with Prenatal Care

Until the seventh month, mom will be going to see the doctor at least once a month. This month's prenatal visit is primarily to check on how mom is doing, to follow up on the results of the initial tests, and possibly to talk about genetic screening. If an ultrasonic exam was not performed during the first visit, mom may undergo her first ultrasound.

Blood Count

If mom's blood count levels were found to be low and she has iron deficiency, her doctor will start her on iron supplementation.

Blood Type

Mom will learn her blood type. If her blood is Rh-negative, the result will probably be a mismatch between her blood and the baby's, and she will likely need additional testing and treatment.

Infections Screening

Most infections that can travel from mom to the baby later in the pregnancy will be identified and treated or monitored. If mom is found to lack antibodies against rubella and chickenpox, she will be advised to avoid people who are infected with these diseases.

First Heart Sounds

By this time, the baby's heart is usually pumping strongly enough that the heartbeat can be heard with a stethoscope. Although they are rare, there are conditions, including certain types of cancers, that can mimic a pregnancy. Finding and hearing the heart indicates that a baby—and not some mimicking condition—is actually present. Every month the doctor will listen to the baby's heartbeat and check its rate.

First Ultrasound

After the eighth week of pregnancy, a vaginal ultrasound exam may be performed to confirm the pregnancy and gestational age, and to determine the number of babies and their location. Not every doctor will order an ultrasound this early in the pregnancy, although many do. Not until later in the pregnancy can an ultrasound exam be used to determine the baby's sex or identify birth defects.

What You Two Should Be Discussing

It is still too early in the pregnancy to know whether everything will be OK with the baby. It is a good idea to remain cautious and not get too excited about the future just yet. For now, it is better to focus on the prenatal care, including the all-important ultrasound that will be performed in week 20.

Genetic Counseling and Testing

Although we have identified numerous genetic diseases, most are relatively rare. Cystic fibrosis is the only disease for which genetic tests are routinely recommended. Tests for other genetic diseases are usually performed only when there is significant risk for them. If certain genes or diseases run in her family or yours, you and mom may be asked to undergo testing to see whether you also have those genes. Deciding whether to participate in genetic counseling and testing can be difficult. Nobody likes to think they may have passed on a potentially dangerous illness to their baby.

Genes

All of our genetic information is contained in series of molecules called deoxyribonucleic acids (DNA). Groupings of DNA that lead to the creation and regulation of a single protein or other molecule are called genes. Each gene usually has two copies—one from the father and one from the mother. It has been estimated that humans have between 20,000 and 100,000 functional genes, but no one knows for sure.

Chromosomes

Genes are packaged into large structures called chromosomes. We inherit a set of 23 chromosomes from each parent, so we have a total of 46 chromosomes. From a distance, the chromosomes in a pair look the same, but on the level of the individual genes, they can differ significantly.

Sex Chromosomes

Two of our 46 chromosomes are called the sex chromosomes because they determine our sex. Males have an X chromosome and a Y chromosome (XY), whereas females have two X chromosomes (XX). Each parent passes on only one sex chromosome (as is the case with other chromosomes) to the baby. Because women have only X chromosomes to give, the sex of the baby is determined by the man. If you passed on an X chromosome, the baby will be a girl. If you passed on a Y chromosome, the baby will be a boy. Occasionally, there is a mix-up with the sex chromosomes, but fortunately this is rare.

Do You Want to Know the Sex?

Although the first ultrasound won't tell you the baby's sex, the second one (at about week 20) will, so you and mom have until the fifth month to decide whether you want to know the baby's sex. Many people want to know as soon as possible because they can't stand the suspense or because the information will help them be better prepared. Knowing whether the baby is a boy or a girl can help in choosing a name.

One of the times when you may have to take over is during active labor, when she is in intense pain, and is scared and fatigued. Your role as her birth coach, or advocate, will be particularly important at this time. Another time might be during the few weeks after the baby is born, when she will be sleep deprived and exhausted.

Some people feel that knowing their child's sex too early takes away some of the mystery and fun. They would rather be surprised. If this is the approach you and mom choose, you will have to take care that no one inadvertently spoils the surprise. Your doctor and many of the medical staff will know the baby's sex even if you don't. With all the patients they work with, it is likely that they could forget that you don't want to know, so be sure to remind them frequently.

What You Should Be Asking Yourself

Many expectant mothers become absolutely obsessed with their pregnancy and want to know everything they can about what is going on. At some point, mom will probably have bought several different pregnancy books, scoured an untold number of Web sites, absorbed countless episodes of birthing shows on TV, and talked at length with tens if not hundreds of other women about it. It will seem to you that by the time the baby is born, mom should qualify for a PhD!

Do I Need to Understand Everything That's Going On?

You may not be all that interested in learning the details of pregnancy, and it may seem that it really isn't necessary to. If mom is throwing herself into the pregnancy, you may be asking whether you need to do so as well. Despite any reticence you may have, it will serve you well to have a good understanding of what's going on, even if you feel "there isn't anything for you to do."

Am I Ready to Make Decisions?

Ideally, you and mom are making all the decisions together. However, it is more likely that mom will be making many of the decisions on her own. This may be OK with you, but there may be times when mom finds it difficult to make decisions on her own. So it is important that you be prepared to take over decision-making responsibilities when necessary. The more you know and the more you are involved, the better prepared you will be.

What You Should Be Doing

The pregnancy can seem pretty complicated during the first few months. There are a few things you could be doing to help you get past the learning curve and get involved.

Tell Her You Want to Know What's Going On

Make it clear to your partner from the beginning that you are interested in being in the loop and a full partner in the decision-making process. Fight the tendency to delegate everything to her.

Set Regular "Study Dates"

Set time aside at least once a week for both of you to go to the library to learn more about the pregnancy. She can read her books, and you can read this one. When either of you has a question, you can try to answer it together.

Schedule Time for Important Prenatal Visits

You may not be able to attend every prenatal visit, especially toward the end as they increase in frequency, but you should at least make the important ones. Find out which visits are important to mom and set the time aside in advance.

Make It a Habit to Review Test Results Together

It's a good idea to sit down after each prenatal visit to talk about any tests the doctor may have ordered and to discuss the significance of results that may have come back. If you aren't sure why a procedure was ordered or what the results mean, then you should work together to figure it out or remember to ask the doctor on the next visit.

Keep Track of the Changes

Create a binder or spreadsheet and start tracking the changes mom is going through. Imagine that you are conducting a research project, and quantify your notes and observations as much as you can. Not only will this make you interested in staying involved, it will also help you better appreciate what mom is going through.

14

Month 4

The fourth month of the pregnancy starts with week 14 and ends after week 17. It is the start of the second trimester, which is a very happy time for most pregnant women. Many of the early symptoms of pregnancy will be lessening, and it is usually safe to start widely telling people you are expecting a baby. This month marks the beginning of what many women consider the honeymoon period of the pregnancy.

What's Happening with the Baby

By this point, the baby is starting to shift from creating new organs and body structures to developing and maturing those already in place. The placenta has formed and begun to take over production of the pregnancy hormones; it now connects the baby's circulatory system to that of the mother. Having access to the mother's blood is critical to start the baby's growth spurt. However, it also means that the baby is exposed to toxins and infections from the mother. By the end of this month, the baby is about 6 inches long and weighs about 4 or 5 ounces.

What May Be Happening with Her

The pregnancy hormone surge will start to level off and she should be starting to feel much better. Her morning sickness will be fading, her energy level should be starting to return to normal, and her interest in sex may rekindle. She may notice that her breasts are getting larger and that she is gaining some weight, about 5 or 10 pounds. Her uterus may also be enlarging to the point that she is "starting to show."

Weight Gain

Although mom's weight gain will come in spurts, it can be compared with expected values for her height and the baby's gestational age to assess how things are going. Gaining too much can be just as harmful as gaining too little.

Breast Enlargement

Mom's breasts are going to continue to get bigger as the milk glands increase in size and fat builds up in preparation for breastfeeding.

The average weight gain during a normal pregnancy is 25–35 pounds. For women who are overweight at the start of pregnancy, the average weight gain is 15–25 pounds. For women who are underweight at the start of pregnancy, the average weight gain is 28–40 pounds.

Skin Changes

Pregnant women can experience many different types of skin changes. Depending on how much mom values having her skin looking its best, she will respond to these changes with emotions that can range from mild annoyance to great distress.

Forgetfulness

You may start noticing that mom is becoming more forgetful. It is not clear whether this is caused by hormonal changes, stress, fatigue, or sleeping problems, but it is common. This is another reason to help her with errands and to otherwise simplify her life.

What You Can Expect

Now that mom is feeling better, the prenatal activity is settling down, and you are thinking about the future, you are likely to experience a lot of different emotions. Many of them will center on your role as provider and protector of the family.

Fears of Not Being Able to Provide

One of the first things a man thinks about when he is told he is going to be a father is how he is going to pay for it all. The financial stresses of having a baby, particularly the first, can be enormous. There is no doubt that it is expensive to have and raise children. The younger and less established you are in your job or career, the more concerned you will be. Careful analysis of your finances and the development of a money management plan can help alleviate some of your fears.

Men have been hunters and gatherers for thousands of years, so it is not surprising that most expectant fathers become focused during pregnancy on the financial issues.

Feelings of Panic

There will be times when you will be hit with sudden anxiety. In fact, it may hit you with such force that you feel panicky. This is perfectly natural and tends to happen with increasing frequency as the due date approaches. It may produce a sense of paralysis on one extreme, and a will to flee on the other. Neither is helpful and both can have long-term consequences. When you experience these feelings, try to recognize what they are and realize that they will inevitably pass. The key is not to do or say anything stupid. It may be a good idea to talk it out with someone other than your partner. You may find that talking out loud about your feelings and fears helps diminish the anxiety and allows you to regain control.

Feeling Overprotective

For thousands of years, men have had to physically protect their families from the environment, ferocious animals, and other humans. Biology has facilitated this role by making men larger, stronger, and more prone to violence than women. So don't be surprised if you sometimes find yourself harboring irrational fears about something posing a danger to your new family, or if you experience strong urges to defend mom and new baby. It is important to recognize what is a real threat and what is not.

What's Going on with Prenatal Care

Now that the baby is past the critical first three months of development, the chances of a miscarriage are drastically reduced. However, it is still possible that the baby may suffer a birth defect. Starting in the fourth month, it is possible for your doctor to remove a sample of mom's amniotic fluid to test for certain genetic and chromosomal defects. This procedure is called an amniocentesis. Although it is generally very safe, it does carry the real risk of causing a miscarriage. So unless your doctor has a good reason to perform an amniocentesis, blood tests and an ultrasound are preferred as screening techniques for birth defects. If the results of these other tests are negative, the chance of your baby having Down's syndrome or some other birth defect is very low.

Alpha-Fetoprotein Test (AFP)

The AFP test is a blood test that screens for abnormalities like Down's syndrome or a neural tube defect like spina bifida. If the test is positive it may be repeated, or a triple-screen test may be ordered. In most cases, the results are a false positive, and no problem is found.

Triple-Screen Test

The triple-screen test uses two additional blood measurements to improve the accuracy of the alpha-fetoprotein test. It is often used to follow up on an abnormal AFP test outcome. Abnormal values of all three tests increase the odds that something may be wrong, but they still don't prove it.

Nuchal Translucency

Nuchal translucency is a special finding seen on an ultrasound. If it is found in addition to an abnormal triple-screen test, there is a high risk of Down's syndrome. Being able to identify this condition requires special skill and testing apparatus.

> Because the results of these screening tests are frequently positive even when nothing is wrong (a false positive test result), they can lead to a lot of unnecessary fear and anxiety. So remember that if the doctor says that the results of one or more of the screening tests are "positive," the odds are still heavily in your favor that everything will turn out all right for the baby.

Amniocentesis

Amniocentesis involves removing amniotic fluid to test for genetic diseases and chromosomal abnormalities. It can be performed to follow up on abnormal results from screening tests or when there is significant risk based on family history or the mother's age.

What You Two Should Be Discussing

Now that mom is feeling better and it is safe to talk about the future, this is the perfect time to discuss the family's finances. Having a baby is expensive. So, unless you are fabulously wealthy, addressing money issues with mom is probably going to be stressful. Before you two start thinking about all the things you need to buy for the baby, you should perform an organized and detailed analysis of your finances. By doing this, you will make sure you both have the same realistic understanding of your family's financial health.

> If a baby is at very high risk for having genetic problems, chorionic villus sampling (CVS) can be performed as early as week 9 of the pregnancy. The benefit of performing CVS instead of amniocentesis is the earlier diagnosis, but there is a real risk of causing a miscarriage or limb damage.

What Are Your Financial Assets?

A financial asset is something that can be used to make purchases now or in the future. The most obvious asset is the money in the bank that you have immediate access to, such as checking accounts, savings accounts, or money market accounts. Next are investment assets that can be converted to cash relatively quickly, such as stocks, bonds, and mutual funds in taxable investment accounts. You can include the money in your retirement accounts, but keep in mind that you may not be able to access this without a significant penalty. To be conservative, you should not include the equity in your home or business, or the resale value of consumer items such as cars, jewelry, or electronics. The reason is that until you actually sell your house, business, or other item, it has no cash value. Today's price for something doesn't mean that you can sell it for the same price tomorrow.

What Are Your Financial Liabilities?

A financial liability is some sort of debt or loan that has to be repaid and should be repaid as soon as possible. The most common liabilities are credit card debt, car loans, and school loans. Mortgage loans are not included because you didn't include the value of your house in the estimate of your assets. It is crucial to pay off credit card debt because of the high interest rates. It is equally important to pay off auto loans because cars depreciate in value extremely quickly. Do not be tempted to borrow money against the value of your home, assuming that housing prices will continue to rise. Despite the tax advantages that may be available, home equity loans should probably be paid off as soon as possible, and are considered a liability.

What Is Your Net Worth?

Now that you have figured out your assets and liabilities, it is time to figure out your current net worth. As you calculate your net worth by subtracting your liabilities from your assets, keep in mind what you are trying to find out. The calculation is not intended to be a scorecard so that you can compare yourself to others. Its purpose is to give you a feel for your ability to withstand an unexpected expense or loss of

Your financial health is determined not solely by your net worth but also by how fast your net worth is changing. For example, if you are just out of school with a lot of school debt but have a high-income job, you are probably in better shape than someone with no debt who is unemployed with little savings. In addition to financial reserve, you want to know your rate of saving or not saving.

income. Your net worth will affect your ability to make large purchases in the future. Estimating your net worth can help motivate you to pay off your debt as soon as possible (pay the highest-interest accounts first).

Are You Saving or Losing Money?

The quickest way to answer this question is to compare the balances of your savings and investments over a given period of time, typically 6–12 months. Because your goal is to assess your ability to save—or at least not spend—you need to correct for the appreciation of your investments. This is better than focusing on deposits or contributions you made, because it accounts for any increases in spending. Although it is great when your investments increase in value, there is no guarantee that the growth will continue, despite what financial analysts tell you.

What You Should Be Asking Yourself

Many expectant fathers become overly focused on the need to make money to provide for their families. Although having an income is important, it is not important to the exclusion of everything else.

What Does It Mean to Provide for Your Family?

As an expectant father, you need to make sure that mom and the baby have the basic necessities. This means making sure there is enough nutritious food, safe housing, adequate clothing, and health care. Then you need to think about such other big expenses as medical necessities, a bigger car or house, the baby's furniture, and other, less obvious costs such as diapers, formula, health insurance, and life insurance. However, you also need to realize that being a father means more than making money to buy things. Sure, you need to provide the basic necessities, but how much do they really need beyond that? Just as it is true that money can't buy you happiness, neither can it buy happiness for your children.

Am I Focusing Enough Attention on Her?

Many women become particularly emotional, complaining, and even needy during pregnancy. Many expectant fathers, already dealing with their own anxiety, can find this overwhelming. Their natural instinct may be to disengage and withdraw during the pregnancy and to reactively reengage only when necessary, such as when there's a problem or a crisis, or when the baby is about to be born. Paradoxically, this approach is usually counterproductive, as it makes him less involved in the pregnancy and leaves her feeling more isolated and insecure.

Paying attention to her is psychologically important to both of you. It can prevent an emotional crisis from forming and can give you a sense of purpose and accomplishment. One of the best ways of doing this is by being a patient listener when she expresses her emotions and complaints. Instead of trying to solve the problem in order to get past it, focus on trying to understand why she has the fears and worries that she does. Try not to dismiss what may seem the "silliness" of her concern. Instead, reassure and encourage her.

Showing her that you care with small gifts and compliments will go a long way. Whatever the approach, if your focus is on her, it will make things go much more smoothly. There is wisdom in the adage "An ounce of prevention is worth a pound of cure."

What You Should Be Doing

Although now is a good time to start assessing your finances it should not be to the exclusion of everything else. Here are a few other things you could be doing as well.

Tell Your Friends and Family

If you haven't already done so, by now it is generally safe to let people know that you are going to be a father. Once you make it past the first trimester, the odds of having a healthy baby go up dramatically.

Tell Her She Is Beautiful

Although she may not be "showing" yet, mom will have noticed her weight gain and begun to wonder whether you still find her attractive. Make sure to let know that you still find her just as beautiful, or more.

Start Keeping Track of Your Expenses

If you aren't sure where all your money is going, start keeping track of your expenses. You should have a good idea of where your money is going within one or two months.

Check Your Credit History

In making preparations for the baby, you may need to apply for the credit to pay for this life-changing event, especially if you want to get a mortgage loan. This would be a good time to find out your credit score and to "clean up" your credit report if necessary. This means correcting any mistakes and having outdated material removed.

Start Paying Off Debt

Having and raising children is going to be expensive. If you are already in debt, it may be hard to make ends meet later. Now is the time to cut back on discretionary spending and start paying off your debt.

Shop for Maternity Clothes with Her

Even if you don't like shopping, it will let her know that you are focused on her and thinking about her needs. It will also show that, despite your concerns about the looming expenses of fatherhood, you are prepared to buy her what she needs.

15

Month 5

The fifth month of the pregnancy starts with week 18 and ends after week 21. It is halfway through the second trimester, and it is an important milestone in the pregnancy. This is the month when the baby is first clearly recognizable on ultrasound and when it is possible to found out if it is a boy or a girl.

What's Happening with the Baby

At this point, the baby is entering a period of accelerated growth and physical activity. He will be spending a lot of time turning from side to side, grabbing at the umbilical cord, and punching and kicking. The amniotic sac that surrounds him is growing and giving him the room he needs to move. He is also starting to develop a sleep pattern, with more regular periods of waking and catnaps. By the end of this month, he will be about 10 inches long and weigh about 1 pound.

What May Be Happening with Her

Except for the occasional pregnancy-related annoyance, such as a bloody nose or bleeding gums, mom should still be feeling pretty good. Her uterus will have extended to the level of her belly button, and she may be starting to feel the baby moving around and kicking. If this is her first pregnancy, she might not be sure what it is. By the end of this month, mom will have likely gained between 10 and 15 pounds, and if she wasn't wearing maternity clothes before, she'll probably start to now.

> For some women, the transition from being able to fit in her old clothes to having to wear maternity clothes can be troubling. They feel fat because they have gained weight and lost their figure, but they are not so large that it is obvious they are pregnant.

Nosebleeds

Being pregnant causes a woman to increase the amount of blood in her body. This can lead the small blood vessels in the nose to occasionally break, especially if they are dry. Using a humidifier or placing a small amount of petroleum jelly under her nose before going to bed can sometimes help relieve the dryness.

Bleeding Gums

Pregnancy can cause mom's gums to swell up, be sore, or bleed during brushing or flossing. It might be annoying to her, but unless she has gingivitis, there isn't much that can be done.

Leaky Breasts

You might notice that mom's breasts are leaking some fluid, especially during sexual arousal or breast massage. This usually occurs later in the pregnancy, but it can happen earlier. This fluid is called colostrum; if your partner breastfeeds, it will be used as nourishment by the baby for the first few days after birth.

Vaginal Discharge

Mom's cervix is making fluids that help keep the vagina clean. If the fluid becomes darker or foul smelling, it may be a sign of an infection that needs to be treated. Bright red blood is always a concern, and mom needs to tell her doctor if it appears.

What You Can Expect

Even though the pregnancy is half over, you probably haven't yet come to terms with all the changes you are going to be experiencing when the baby is born.

Worries That You Are Not Going to Have Enough Help

Having a baby and raising a family is harder for parents these days. In the past, most parents lived close to their families and had extended relatives to help out. Today it is not uncommon for new parents to be on their own, having relocated for work or some other reason. This can put a tremendous amount of strain on you, especially if you're both working. Thinking about how you and mom can arrange for help after the baby arrives is a very good idea.

Occasional Disappointment

Having a baby is a time of great expectations. If you find that you are disappointed about something, you should be considerate of mom's feelings in the matter.

Wondering if Sex Is Going to Change after the Baby Arrives

The status of sex is a topic of intense interest to newly expectant fathers. Although many people have written about sex and pregnancy, and no doubt it is a topic that deserves its own book, this isn't it. Many of the other pregnancy books talk about how you and your partner's interest in sex will either increase or decrease. The truth is that your partner's desire for sex and the amount you have cannot be predicted from a book. However, it is true that a significant number of women lose some interest in sex after the baby is born. This is probably due in part to the perpetual fatigue and lack of sleep. So unless you are fabulously wealthy, with lots of time to relax, several nannies to take of your kids, and servants to take care of the rest, she (and you) will often be tired during this time.

What's Going on with Prenatal Care

This month's prenatal visit is particularly important, and you should try very hard not to miss it. Not only do you get your first really good look at the baby on ultrasound and receive a picture, you can also tell whether it is going to be a boy or girl, if you've decided that you want to know. Since it is still a little hard to tell what everything is, the doctor or ultrasound technician will point out where the different body parts are.

After the ultrasound, the prenatal visits become routine, at least until it gets close to the due date. The main reason to continue to have frequent prenatal visits is to make sure that the pregnancy is progressing as expected and to monitor for complications.

Blood Pressure Check

Mom's blood pressure will be checked every visit, even if she doesn't normally have a problem with high blood pressure. Rises in blood pressure during pregnancy may be sign of preeclampsia, a serious disorder that often requires labor to be induced and the baby delivered as soon as possible. The doctor will be looking more at the changes in blood pressure than at the actual blood pressure itself.

Baby's Heart Rate

The baby's heartbeat is an important indicator of how well he is doing, and it will be routinely checked during the prenatal period. A normal fetal heart rate is generally between 120 and 160 beats per minute.

Fundal Height

The fundal height is the distance from the top of the pubic bone to the top of the uterus, measured in centimeters. It is measured to get a rough idea of how the baby is growing and if there is enough amniotic fluid. After week 20, the height is roughly equal to the gestational age in weeks. However, this relationship is not always accurate, especially when there are twins or triplets.

The easiest way to "hear" the baby's heartbeat is by using a fetal Doppler heart monitor. It sends out small, high-frequency sound waves that are reflected back and amplified. Each time there is a beat, the monitor makes a swooshing sound.

Urine Screening

Mom's urine will be checked on this and every other visit for signs of diabetes, urinary traction infections, or preeclampsia. All three are known to cause complications during pregnancy.

What You Two Should Be Discussing

If this is your first baby, it is very likely that both of you have jobs and careers. Now that a baby is on the way, you need to talk about how it is going to affect either or both of your careers. For a woman, trying to decide between keeping her career or staying at home to raise her children can be one of the most difficult decisions of the pregnancy. You need to spend time talking about what it means to her to be a mother and what her expectations are for work once the baby is born. You should also discuss whether it makes more sense for you to stay home and for her to work.

> If the maternity leave is unpaid, you may need to be tactful when discussing how much time she is going to take off. She shouldn't feel that you are pushing her to go back to work because of the money.

If mom does plan on continuing her job or career, she will need to arrange for maternity leave. It is customary for women to take six weeks off for a vaginal birth and eight weeks for a cesarean section, but some companies offer more time off. Some women want to take as much time as they can, whereas others want to get back to work as soon as possible.

What You Should Be Asking Yourself

Even if things are going pretty well, you should still periodically evaluate your involvement to make sure you are living up to your responsibilities as the expectant father.

Are We Talking Enough?

Disagreements on important decisions or mismatched expectations between partners have a way of escalating during times of high stress and anxiety. To avoid serious conflicts during the pregnancy and after the baby is born, it is important for you and mom to deal with them early, before they become a problem. Even if you have no opinion on an issue, or she has a particularly strong one, it is important to be engaged in the discussion. It not only keeps you more involved, but also shows her that you're interested in what she thinks.

Am I Encouraging Her Enough?

Whether it is in sports, business, or one's personal life, most people need encouragement at one time or another to achieve their goals. It is the rare person who doesn't need someone to offer motivation every now and then to help get the job done. One of your roles as the expectant father will be to express enthusiasm and encouragement for the pregnancy. You need to make mom feel that having a baby is the most important thing in the world; however, this doesn't mean you should be so relentlessly enthusiastic that it comes off as being insincere.

Enthusiasm and encouragement are not always enough: frequent compliments and the occasional gift are always appreciated as well, and avoiding unnecessary criticism is also important.

Am I Reducing Our Stress Levels?

Having a baby brings enough stress to any couple. There is no need to add more. It may help to establish a routine and be consistent about it. Try to avoid taking on any new responsibilities that will take up a lot of your time and put you under additional pressure. Of course, this may be easier said than done. Try to keep your emotions under control, and don't let situations get out of hand.

Am I Happy with My Life?

Being a father eventually forces you to realize that you are getting older, and you are not going to be around forever. Many people are blinded to the future by their drive to make money, achieve fame, and accumulate power. They are so busy with their careers that they ignore long-term happiness and their inevitable mortality. Before the baby is born, and while things are relatively simple, you should take the time to evaluate whether you are happy with your career and life. (For example, if you hate your job, now is the time to change it, if possible.) If you are not happy, no matter how much money or power you have, it is going to have a negative affect on your baby. Also, becoming a father can change the way you look at the world. Although it might not happen overnight, you will eventually come to realize that your baby is going to grow up and go out into the world, and you need to enjoy the time you have with him.

What You Should Be Doing

Now that you have finished dealing with the finances and before you start dealing with all the preparations for the baby, it is a good idea to bank some quality time with mom. Things may get a bit bumpier toward the end of the pregnancy and after the baby is born.

Take a Picture of Her Belly

At this point mom might be little self-conscious about her growing belly. She may feel that she looks more fat than pregnant. By wanting to take a picture, you are showing her how excited you are that the baby is starting to show.

Give Her a Special Gift

Buy mom a picture frame for the ultrasound photo, treat her to a massage or beauty treatment, or do some other thing you think she would really like. Tell her it's to celebrate all the changes she is going through for you and the baby.

Tell Her What an Amazing Mother You Think She Will Be

Mom may be very conflicted about wanting to work versus staying at home. You should reassure her that you think she is going to be a great mother, no matter what she decides.

Write the Baby a Letter

After this month's ultrasound, write the baby a letter telling him how excited you are and how you can't wait until he is born. Give the letter to mom and ask her to read it to the baby when you are traveling or away at work.

Review Your Partner's Maternity Policy

If your partner is taking maternity leave, review her company's policy. Pay particular attention to whether it is paid or unpaid leave.

16

Month 6

The sixth month of the pregnancy starts with week 22 and ends after week 26. It is the last month of the second trimester and is the time that new parents usually start thinking about setting up the nursery and making preparations for the baby. Also, by the end of this month, the honeymoon period of pregnancy is drawing to an end.

What's Happening with the Baby

At this point, the baby is on track for a rapid rate and extended period of growth. He will be gaining between 1 and 2 pounds per month until birth, and a good portion of this weight gain is due to the storage of fat that will help regulate his body temperature and keep him warm at birth. To help protect his fragile skin from the amniotic fluid, the baby is covered with fine, soft hair, called *lanugo*, and a cheesy substance, called *vernix*. By the end of the month, the baby is about 12 inches long and weighs about 2 pounds.

What May Be Happening with Her

Mom will be continuing to gain weight, and her uterus will be getting more pronounced. She may be starting to experience mild discomfort from her enlarged belly, but overall she should be feeling good. If she didn't notice or recognize it before, she should definitely be feeling the baby moving around and kicking by now. Also, since the due date is getting closer, you will probably notice that mom is becoming more concerned about getting your home ready for the baby.

Pelvic Pressure

The enlarging uterus can put a lot of pressure on mom's pelvis. There can be pain from the stretching of the ligaments supporting the uterus or from the pinching of the nerves passing by it to her legs. If changing positions doesn't relieve the pressure, you might give her a hot compress or a massage.

Itchy Skin

As the uterus enlarges, the skin will stretch over it. This can lead to some abdominal itching, especially if the skin is already dry. Using moisturizers might help the dry skin, but it may not take away all the itching.

Stretch Marks

Stretch marks are scar tissue caused by over-stretching of the skin. They are more common toward the end of pregnancy but can start sooner, depending on how big the uterus already is. They can be very distressing for a woman, but there is no good way to prevent them. Buying expensive moisturizers or creams for her won't help with the stretch marks, but it might make her feel better.

Trouble Sleeping

Mom might have problems sleeping at some point during the pregnancy. This is not unusual. She may also be having trouble falling asleep because of disruption in her sleep cycle due to hormones, anxiety, or difficulty getting comfortable. This is particularly common in the eighth and ninth months.

What You Can Expect

With all the talk of making preparations for the baby, you might start getting a little anxious. Many expectant fathers start to feel the way a student does when thinking about final exams looming in the near future.

Growing Confidence

Unless you already have experience with pregnancy, childbirth, and raising children, you are not going to start out with much confidence. But as you develop knowledge and experience, your confidence will grow. This is not to say that issues are not going to come up that might temporarily shake your confidence, but that is likely to be temporary. With each new lesson or mistake, you are going to grow more knowledgeable, experienced, and confident.

Feelings of Incompetence

You and mom are going to be dealing with many things when the baby is born. You will be occupied with cooking, cleaning, changing diapers, and other tasks you may not normally do. Don't be surprised if you don't do a perfect job; feelings of incompetence are common for first-time fathers. Fortunately, with experience and knowledge comes competence. By the time number two comes around, you will be a seasoned pro!

Feelings of Frustration

No doubt your life is fairly complex. You probably have many responsibilities that place you under pressure and stress. Things that disturb you or distract you from what you feel you should be doing may invoke feelings of frustration and anger. This is understandable, but it is not a good idea to act on them or act out because of them. It might make you temporarily feel better, but there is a good chance that mom is not going to react well to it. She may interpret it as a sign that you aren't 100% enthusiastic about having the baby.

Fears of Having Sex

It is not uncommon for an expectant father to have some concern about whether having sex during the pregnancy will hurt the baby. Except when there is some sort of complication, such as improper placement of the placenta or a higher risk for premature birth, most experts consider sex during pregnancy perfectly safe. The uterus and amniotic fluid will act as a shock absorber to protect the baby.

What's Going on with Prenatal Care
- -

Unless mom is experiencing a particularly troubling issue or complication, this month's prenatal visit will be a brief checkup. Since most couples start thinking about signing up for a birthing class about now, this would be a good time for you and mom to talk to her doctor about pain control during natural and traditional forms of childbirth.

Traditional Childbirth

In traditional childbirth, the control of pain is achieved using regional anesthesia. This involves blocking the nerves to a certain area and includes epidural and spinal anesthesia. It doesn't completely take away the pain, but it does lessen it considerably. The main downside is that it can slow down the labor process by decreasing the incentive for the mother to get the baby out sooner. If there is no time to put in an epidural, pain medications may be given through an intravenous line. The risk is that if it is not done carefully, it can cause drowsiness in the mother and the baby as well as dropping the blood pressure.

Natural Childbirth

Over the last couple of decades, there has been a controversy as to what is the best method of pain control during birth. Traditionalists believe in using whatever medications and technology are available, and naturalists want to avoid artificial techniques of pain suppression. Both approaches are considered acceptable for uncomplicated labor. There are a number of different natural or alternative options available, and they are usually taught as part of a childbirth class. Which one is right for you and mom will depend on your particular philosophy concerning pregnancy and childbirth.

What You Two Should Be Discussing

For many women, this month marks the point where they start really thinking about making preparations for the baby. Mom will be thinking about all the things you need to buy, including setting up the nursery and having the essential supplies. These feelings are not going to be limited to your partner, as you too might start feeling the need to get things in order. For many, this is a proactive response to the increasing realization that the baby is almost here.

Going Shopping

Getting things in order at home helps one deal with anxiety and restores a sense of control. However, when you start making a list of the things you will need for the baby, it can be a little overwhelming. Talking with mom about what you truly need and how much you should spend can help keep the costs under control.

Diapers: Disposable versus Cloth

The thought of using anything other than disposable diapers may seem incomprehensible to many new parents. The decision is very easy for them to make. For those who worry about the cost not only to their budgets but also to the environment, it may be a bit more difficult. Disposables are very expensive, even when purchased in bulk. They also are not biodegradable and contribute to filling up many landfills. However, the alternative may not be that much better. Even if you wash cloth diapers at home, there is a significant cost in terms of water and energy. The power plants creating that energy are very likely contributing to air pollution and global warming. If you choose to use the services of diaper cleaning companies, you also have to consider the cost and the environmental consequences of transporting all the diapers to and from your home. At the present time, there is no

Sample Purchases

Baby carrier	$40
Baby clothes	$300
Baby formula	$100
Bassinet	$150
Bathtub	$20
Blanket	$75
Bumper pads	$100
Car seat	$150
Changing table/dresser	$400
Crib	$600
Decorations	$100
Disposable diapers	$100
High chair	$100
Mattress	$100
Mobile	$50
Monitor	$50
Portable playpen	$150
Rocking chair	$150
Sheets	$50
Stroller	$300
Toys	$400
Miscellaneous	$500
Total	$3,985

good alternative for the environment. Hopefully someone will develop a biodegradable disposable diaper soon.

Breastfeeding When Going Back to Work

Breastfeeding can be a sensitive subject for working women. Some feel that using formula amounts to a missed opportunity for bonding and that it is less nutritious for their baby. Once a woman goes back to work, it can be very difficult for her to continue breastfeeding. Although she can use a breast pump to remove the breast milk and place it in bottles to bring home, it can be very difficult to find the time and location to consistently pump at work. If the women don't pump regularly, their breasts will stop producing the milk. There is also the problem of storing the milk at work.

Leave the decision to breastfeed up to her. If she asks, just reassure her that there is nothing wrong with using formula when she goes back to work.

What You Should Be Asking Yourself

With the honeymoon period of pregnancy about to end, you can bet that things are going to be changing soon. Up to this point, have you been involved as much as you should have been? If not, there is still time to make some changes of your own.

Am I Being Sensitive about Her Weight Gain?

Gaining weight is a normal and important part of the pregnancy process. However, many women are very sensitive to how the weight gain will affect their appearance and attractiveness to their partners. For that matter, so are many men. Given the highly charged nature surrounding this issue, it is best to assume that her weight is normal and appropriate, unless she was told by her doctor otherwise. It is smart to err on the side of caution and offer frequent compliments.

Should I Be Thinking about Paternity Leave?

Traditionally, much of the responsibility for taking care of a newborn falls to the mother, but not today. New fathers wanting to spend time at home after the birth have deferred vacation during the pregnancy and saved it up for when the baby is born. However, since the Family and Medical Leave Act of 1993, it is possible for fathers to take paternity leave.

Because the weight gain can come in spurts, it is difficult to know what the "ideal weight" for mom should be from week to week. Mom's doctor will be monitoring her weight using a body mass index chart every time she has an appointment. Using her height and weight along with the gestational age, the doctor can track her weight gain closely.

Even though a few progressive companies have developed paternity leave policies, they are rarely used. Unlike maternity leave, many people consider it unnecessary. Most reasonable bosses and employers expect that you are going to be distracted and less than 100% efficient. However, unless you believe that taking paternity leave is acceptable and truly supported by your employer, you should probably plan on using vacation or sick days when the baby is born.

What You Should Be Doing

The third trimester and the birth are going to be here before you know it. Have you started to get ready, or have you procrastinated?

Try to Feel the Baby Kicking Every Day

Feeling the baby kicking every day can help the two of you form a bond, because it makes it all that much more real to you that there is somebody in there waiting to come out.

Sign up for Childbirth Classes with Her

Birthing classes started as a way of promoting a particular natural childbirth philosophy, so if you are interested in being a birthing coach, this is where you will learn how. Even if you aren't, it will still teach you a lot about labor and delivery.

Help Her Research Her Shopping List for the Baby

There are many things to buy for the baby, and it can take a lot of time and effort to research each brand or model. Not only does it help her out, but the more knowledgeable you are, the more influence you have when it comes to buying or not buying something.

Start an Emergency Fund

Ideally, you should have saved up enough money to cover at least six months of expenses. If you don't have this much available, you should start setting aside money in an emergency fund.

Arrange a Quick Getaway

During the last two months of pregnancy, mom will need to stay near her doctor and won't be able to travel. Before this happens, you should arrange a weekend getaway this month or next.

17

Month 7

The seventh month of the pregnancy starts with week 27 and ends with week 30. It is the first month of the third trimester and, for many women, the month that they start to experience the effects from their rapidly expanding uterus. This month marks the official end of the honeymoon period and the beginning of the final stretch.

What's Happening with the Baby

At this point the baby is still growing fast, and his space is starting to get cramped. With less room to move, his punches and kicks will be less energetic. He is also starting to be able hear sounds around him, but they are muffled, just like when you are listening underwater. Nonetheless, he is starting to recognize mom's heartbeat and your voices. By the end of this month, he will be about 15–16 inches long and weigh 3 pounds. Although he could probably survive if he were born now, his lungs would be immature.

What May Be Happening with Her

Mom will be continuing to gain about a pound a week and should be getting quite big by now. Her uterus is starting to push its way back down into her pelvic area, so it might be causing her some problems soon, especially with her bladder. Also, she will probably be more fatigued from the effort it takes to carry around the extra weight and possible difficulty sleeping.

Backache

Having some backache during pregnancy is normal and understandable. The extra weight of pregnancy combined with changes in posture can put strain on the muscles and ligaments in mom's back.

Later in pregnancy, backache may be a sign of preterm labor, especially if she hasn't had much of a problem with it earlier. Severe pain is not normal and may mean that she has a pinched nerve, kidney stone, or infection.

Leg Cramps

Leg cramps are caused by the sudden tightening of muscles and can lead to intense pain. They tend to occur during the last few months of pregnancy and particularly at night. It is not clear why they occur, but it may have to do with stress on the legs or on the nerves and the blood vessels going to them.

If the leg cramps involve only one leg, and it has warmth, redness, pain, or swelling out of proportion to the other, mom could have a blood clot, and she should call her doctor immediately. Leg cramps usually go away on their own, but until they do, they are excruciatingly painful.

Clumsiness

The increased weight and unusual distribution of the baby and uterus alter a pregnant woman's center of gravity. During the last couple of months of the pregnancy, she has a higher risk of losing her balance and falling.

Overheating

Pregnant women have a hard time dealing with heat and humidity. They just aren't able to get rid of the extra heat as efficiently as nonpregnant women. In mild cases, overheating can be uncomfortable. It moderate cases, it can lead to fainting. In severe cases, it can lead to cardiovascular collapse and death.

Faintness

During pregnancy a woman's blood vessels relax to make room for the extra blood she is making. This tends to lower her blood pressure and makes her prone to fainting. This happens when she stands up quickly, because it is harder for her blood vessels to keep the blood from rushing to her feet and away from her head. This can be made worse if she is overheated or dehydrated.

What You Can Expect

For the last couple of months mom has probably been feeling pretty good. Now that she is starting to have some symptoms again, including fatigue, backache, or difficulty sleeping, she might start getting a little moody because of the discomfort.

Love for Your Baby

Love usually grows as a result of emotional bonding. For a woman who carries a baby around with her for nine months, it is easier to bond. For the expectant father, it can be more challenging. If you aren't feeling affection for the baby as much as you thought you would, don't worry; it will come in time, especially after the baby is born. At some point you will have that feeling of wanting to do anything and everything for your child.

Feelings of Isolation

It is inevitable that others' attention will be focused on mom. If you are used to having all eyes on you, this may a little hard to get used to. If you do feel isolated, at least try to enjoy it. When the baby comes, you are going to find your free time diminished. If you are feeling jealous that mom is not paying enough attention to you, again get used to it. Once the baby is born, you are definitely going to be number two on mom's list of important people, and that is the way it should be.

Fear about Handling the Stress

No doubt you have already realized that having a baby is stressful. In and of itself, the stress is not a problem if you don't get overwhelmed and paralyzed by it. In fact, a proper amount of stress can motivate you and make you efficient. Just keep in mind that it is extremely unlikely that you are going to experience something that hasn't been felt by countless other fathers. The key to dealing with stress is proper preparation, staying focused, and getting enough rest.

It helps to keep in mind that crying is *supposed* to make you uncomfortable; it's the baby's primary method of getting your attention and making you do something. With time, you and mom will learn why the baby cries and what to do to make him stop.

Fear about Handling the Crying

There is no doubt that a crying baby can get on your nerves. If you've ever spent an extended period of time trapped next to a colicky baby on a plane, you know that it can be uncomfortable. Fortunately, the cries of your own baby are a lot less irritating than those of other people's kids. However, there are certain times when it can really test the limit of your patience. For example, it can be difficult when it happens in the middle of the night, you are exhausted, and you don't know what is wrong. This is particularly likely during the first couple of months. Another difficult time is when the baby experiences colic, or uncontrollable crying. Colic is thought to be due to gas, and there doesn't seem to be any effective treatment.

What's Going on with Prenatal Care

Starting this month, mom will be going to her prenatal visits at least every other week. She will also be undergoing tests to see if she is experiencing or prone to a form of diabetes called gestational diabetes. This involves having her drink a sugary solution and measuring her blood sugar levels. She is also likely to have additional blood work done to make sure she hasn't developed any infections that pose a risk to the baby.

Glucose Tolerance Testing

Testing for glucose tolerance involves two parts. First mom has her blood level checked an hour after drinking a glucose solution. If the level is normal, the testing is over. If the level is elevated, mom may be asked to repeat the test, but with a different solution and more blood work.

Screening for Infections

Screening for infections now will be very similar to the procedure performed during the first prenatal visit. It is repeated because the doctor needs to make sure that nothing has happened since then.

RhoGAM

If mom is Rh-negative and she doesn't already have antibodies against the Rh blood marker, she will receive the medication RhoGAM now and following the delivery. It is designed to keep her from developing those antibodies, thus protecting her future babies.

What You Two Should Be Discussing

The birth is only three months away! Now is the time to start thinking about a name and where the baby is going to sleep. Although these sound like easy decisions to make, you would be surprised at how difficult they can be sometimes.

Picking a Name

Picking a name can be very easy. For example, the two of you might have already agreed that you want to honor a particular person, or that you like the idea of a junior. However, it is not uncommon for a couple to have a hard time coming up with something that they can agree on. If you don't already have a name that you are dying to use, each of you could come up with a list of names that you like. One person can then veto names on the other's list. Common reasons to veto include already knowing someone with that name, the name is too bland or unusual, or it could result in teasing. Sooner or later you are going to come up with a couple of names that are acceptable to you both. If you are lucky, you two will settle on a name that you really like. If not, don't worry; over time you will get so used to the name that you can't imagine your child having any other one.

Where the Baby Is Going to Sleep

In many cultures babies do not have their own cribs, let alone their own bedrooms. An increasing number of people are advocating having a "family bed," where the baby sleeps in the bed with the parents. It is thought by some that this promotes family bonding and closeness. When the baby is a newborn and breastfeeding, it is certainly a convenience for the mother to be able to turn over and feed the baby without having to turn on the lights or get out of bed.

Despite the benefits, there are some serious downsides to having the baby sleep in your bed. Although it is often overblown, there is a real risk of rolling onto the baby and suffocating him, especially if one of you is a very heavy sleeper. Another concern is whether you will be getting good sleep. Is your bed big enough for all three of you to sleep comfortably? Are you so worried that you are going to roll over on the baby that you are not sleeping as soundly?

> **Another thing to consider when thinking about having the baby sleep with you is what happens when the baby gets older. In my experience, it is good for both the baby and the parents when the baby has his own crib. Otherwise, the baby may not learn to sleep alone.**

What You Should Be Asking Yourself

Having a baby is going to bring you many new responsibilities. In order to meet them, you may have to make some changes to your priorities.

Am I Ready for New Responsibilities?

Having your own family means having new and important responsibilities. Once the baby is born, he will be utterly dependent on you and mom for survival. No doubt you realize this. However, what you may not yet appreciate is how awesome your new responsibilities are. You are responsible not simply for making sure he stays alive, but also for his growing up a happy, productive, considerate, and tolerant person. The moment you hold your new baby will be the moment you realize just how substantial your new responsibilities truly are.

Am I Ready to Change My Priorities?

Not long after you accept your new responsibilities, you are going to realize that you have to make some changes to your priorities. Until now, you probably thought of things only in terms of yourself and your partner. It is a hard habit to break. From the moment you were born, somebody took care of you, and you were the center of attention. Even now that you are grown up and have started a life with someone else, your priorities may still be focused on you. Your partner and your parents are likely to be healthy and independent enough that they don't entirely depend on you. Until someone is absolutely dependent on you, it's only natural that your priorities be centered mainly on yourself.

Your new responsibilities as a father mean that you have to shift your priorities so that the emphasis is on your family and not you. Not every father truly appreciates this, and quite a few families have fallen apart as a result.

What You Should Be Doing

Buying a crib and getting the nursery ready aren't the only preparations you should be making. There are a few other things you could be doing before the baby arrives.

Plan a Dinner and a Show

You should be enjoying some nights out on the town with mom, especially while there is just the two of you, and you don't need to find a sitter.

Start Talking to the Baby Every Night before Bed

Start talking regularly to the baby after you turn out the lights. It will help you bond with him, and it may help him get used to your voice.

Apply for Life and Disability Insurance

If you don't already have insurance, or your employer's coverage isn't adequate, you should start the application process now. Although it doesn't normally take long to get it, sometimes it can take a while if the insurance company has concerns about your medical history, physical exam, or test results.

Review Your Insurance Policies

Take some time to review your current insurance policies, and make sure you really understand them, especially the coverage and restriction details. You will have more time now to meet with your insurance agent to discuss your policies and to make any changes than you will after the baby is born. Also, consider such supplemental policies as umbrella insurance or flood insurance.

Make a Will

If something happens to both you and mom after the baby is born, you will need to have your wishes available in writing. It is particularly important to identify a guardian for your children, especially if you have a sizable estate or life insurance policy.

Check or Install Smoke Detectors

Smoke detectors are an easy, inexpensive, and effective way to protect you and your family from needless harm caused by a fire.

Get Your Traveling Done Now

The risk of mom going into early or preterm labor is higher during the eighth or ninth month than it is now. If you need to make a business trip or travel for another reason, now is the time to do it.

18

Month 8

The eighth month of pregnancy starts with week 31 and ends with week 35. Although you are only halfway through the third trimester, the baby could come at any time.

What's Happening with the Baby

The baby is still growing rapidly, and he is quickly becoming too big to move around much. However, he can still do a fair amount of rolling around and kicking. Fortunately, his umbilical cord is covered with a material to help prevent it from kinking and getting knotted. At this point most of the baby's organs are well formed, but his brain and lungs are continuing to develop. By the end of the month the baby will be 18–19 inches long and about 4–5 pounds.

What May Be Happening with Her

By now mom's uterus is so big that it is starting to push underneath her rib cage and crowd her lungs. This is in addition to all the pressure that it is exerting on her stomach and bladder. Not surprisingly, she might be complaining of shortness of breath, heartburn, and having to go the bathroom all the time. You will probably also notice that she is having a hard time getting comfortable, especially at night. Mom may also be experiencing irregular contractions, called Braxton-Hicks contractions. They are the body's way of warming up for the birth, and they do not mean that mom is going into labor.

Shortness of Breath

Toward the end of the pregnancy, shortness of breath is usually caused by the uterus compressing the lungs. Changing positions, especially becoming upright, or placing pillows under the head can help relieve some of the pressure.

Heartburn

As the uterus starts to press on the stomach, partially digested food and stomach acids can be more easily pushed back up into the esophagus. Certain foods can worsen this by making the valve between the esophagus and the stomach leaky. Common offenders include greasy or fatty foods, spicy foods, large meals, caffeine, and chocolate.

Frequent Urination

If you thought mom's bladder was small before, it is much smaller now with the uterus pressing on it. The amount of urine she is making hasn't really changed, but she has to urinate a lot more just to get rid of it. When you two are out of the house, you should keep an eye out for the nearest bathroom at all times.

Leg Edema

Swelling of the legs is an annoying but normal part of pregnancy. Unlike the case for nonpregnant women, it does not necessarily mean that there is anything wrong with her heart, liver, or kidneys. Standing up a lot during the day and wearing restrictive clothing can impede the blood flow returning from her legs to her heart and can worsen the edema.

What You Can Expect

Now that the birth is only two months away, you can expect to get a little pensive and introspective. Some of the feelings you have been experiencing may have left you wondering what kind of father you are going to be.

A New Sense of Purpose

Some people feel a lack a purpose in their lives. They may have invested a lot of time and energy in the pursuit of money, power, and reputation, only to end up realizing that it doesn't help. You may find that having a baby can provide you with a new purpose—being a good father.

Occasional Feelings of Selfishness

It may shock you to hear this, but you are selfish! In fact, everyone is selfish. It is human nature for you to perform actions that primarily benefit yourself. If this is your first child, you may not have gotten used to thinking about someone else before yourself. So it is not surprising that you still have occasional feelings of selfishness.

Wondering If You Are Going to Be Like Your Father

It is said that the apple doesn't fall far from the tree. There is a certain amount of truth to this. You can't deny that you get half of your genes from your father, and your father probably had a prominent role in your life. This may or may not be a good thing. In either case, if your idea of being a parent differs radically from that of your father, rest assured that you are not destined to be just like him.

What's Going on with Prenatal Care

Mom will be continuing to see the doctor every two weeks. In preparation for birth, a sample from mom's birth canal will be tested to see if a particular bacteria, called group B streptococcus, or GBS, is present. If it is, mom will need to receive antibiotics during labor to keep the baby from being infected with it as he passes through the birth canal. In addition, the doctor may or may not ask for a kick count or nonstress test to assess the baby's well-being. If the pregnancy is considered low risk and things have been going well, it may not be needed.

GBS Culture

Newborns infected with the group B streptococcus can become extremely ill and die shortly after birth. Treatment with antibiotics during labor can prevent this potentially disastrous infection.

Kick Count

The doctor may ask mom to count how many times the baby moves in an hour, or how long it takes for him to move ten times. The doctor usually requests that this be done at home, and the results usually help reassure the doctor about the baby's well-being.

Nonstress Test

The doctor may perform a nonstress test to assess the baby's well-being, especially if the pregnancy is considered high risk. It involves monitoring the baby's heart rate when he is moving. If the heart rate changes appropriately with movement, it is considered *reactive*—and reassuring. If the test is *nonreactive*, the baby is most likely fine, but further testing or monitoring will be necessary.

What You Two Should Be Discussing

Although most babies arrive in the ninth month, it is not uncommon for women to go into early, or preterm, labor. So at this point, it is important for both of you to be prepared for the possibility that the baby could arrive early. This means not only having everything packed and ready to go, but also having a clear idea of what is likely to happen after you arrive at the hospital or birthing center.

When to Call the Doctor

It is not uncommon for new parents to think labor has commenced when it has not. If mom isn't sure if she is or isn't in labor, she should call the doctor and explain her symptoms. It is better to be safe than sorry. Here are some reasons to call the doctor sooner rather than later:

- Her water breaks or her contractions are increasingly frequent, strong, and regular
- There is constant or severe pain
- There is bright red blood or the baby isn't moving as normal
- There is a baby part or the umbilical cord in the vagina (call 911 first)

Making a Birthing Plan

Creating a birthing plan can help mom decide what she wants or doesn't want during the labor and delivery process. Some women put these wishes in writing and give them to the doctor and the hospital. If mom is interested in doing this, she needs to realize that most births don't go exactly as planned. The doctors will have to deviate from her wishes if it comes down to her safety or that of the baby. If she doesn't realize this, she may be setting herself up for feelings of failure and disappointment.

Birth Team

You and mom need to decide who is going to be present during the labor and delivery. It is generally accepted that you will be there and active in the birth, but if she wants somebody else there, you should address this with the doctor in advance.

> If mom wants to put her birthing plan in writing, encourage her to make it a statement of preferences and not a list of demands. Also, it is important that she doesn't outline everything in great detail. Instead, it is better to address issues only where her wishes differ from the routine care provided by her doctor or the hospital.

Labor Preparations

You and mom should discuss whether she plans on refusing any of the labor preparations that are often performed upon admittance to the hospital. In all likelihood, her doctor won't have a problem with her refusing some component of the treatment, as long as it isn't medically necessary.

Baby Monitoring

If mom wants to refuse or limit the use of certain types of baby monitoring, such as external fetal monitoring, you two should first understand what these procedures are for and why they are important. Although a monitor may be somewhat intrusive, it helps keep your baby safe.

Pain Control

Although mom has probably already decided what type of birth she wants, it is important to discuss the possibility that she may change her mind. You should reassure her that if this happens, you will support her no matter what.

Cord Cutting

It is becoming more common for the father to cut the umbilical cord. Most of the time the doctor will ask the father if he wants to, but sometimes she forgets. If this opportunity is important to you, be sure to remind the doctor after the labor has started.

Assisted Labor and Delivery

It is important to realize that most deliveries don't go exactly as planned. Discussing in advance what the doctors may need to do to assist the labor or delivery process can help minimize the disappointment that mom may feel if one of these actions becomes necessary. It is particularly important to discuss how she might feel if it is necessary for her to have a cesarean section.

What You Should Be Asking Yourself

After the baby is born, many of your relationships are going to change. Not surprisingly, the biggest relationship changes will be with your partner and your families.

Am I Ready for the Relationship with My Partner to Change?

It is inevitable that all the changes a baby brings are going to have an effect on your relationships with mom and others. The biggest change will be with mom, because up until now you were probably the focus of her attention. You might have been used to spending a lot of time together, taking vacations, and talking about work, hobbies, or the world. When the baby arrives, you are no longer going to be the most important person in her life. Initially, you might feel isolated and even a little lonely, but as the baby gets older and your relationship with him develops, you will realize how much richer your life is. Until then, get ready to accept that you are no longer the most important person around.

Am I Ready for My Relationships with Our Families to Change?

The baby will be important not only to you and mom but to your families as well. This is especially true if this is the first grandchild in the family. Initially, you may notice that mom is becoming closer to her mother or other women in the family. After the baby is born, you are going to realize that the baby is not just your daughter or son but somebody's granddaughter or niece as well. Whether you want to or not, you are going to be spending more time with your relatives.

What You Should Be Doing

At this point, you need to be prepared for any contingency. If the baby came tonight, would you be prepared? If not, there are a few things you could be doing.

Make Sure the Car Seat Is Installed Correctly

There have been reports suggesting that the majority of car seats are not installed correctly. Take the time to learn how to install it, and find someone to check it.

Prepare Baby Supplies and Essentials

Mom will no doubt have a complete and very long list of things to buy for the baby. Help her double-check that everything is ready and that nothing has been missed.

Pack for the Hospital

Although you probably aren't going to be much help when it comes to packing the clothing and toiletries, you can still help by getting the nonperishable snacks, family photos, portable CD player, and other nonessentials ready.

Help Mom Find a Good Pediatrician

The baby will need to have an appointment with a pediatrician arranged before he is discharged from the hospital. This is particularly important if the baby has a condition that needs treatment or close monitoring.

When looking for a car seat safety inspection program, start with the dealership where you bought your car. If they don't have one, try your local police or fire department.

Take a Tour of the Hospital with Mom

Be sure to accompany mom on her tour of the labor and delivery floor of the hospital or the birthing center. You don't want your first visit to be when mom is going into labor.

19

Month 9

The ninth month of pregnancy starts with week 36 and ends with week 40. It is the last month of the third trimester and, in most cases, the last month of the pregnancy.

What's Happening with the Baby

The baby is still growing rapidly and gaining about a half pound a week. His lungs are now mature and able to function on their own. There is very little room for him to move, but he will still find a way to rotate and drop into a head-down position. By the end of this month, he will be 19–21 inches long and weigh about 6–8 pounds.

What May Be Happening with Her

At this point mom is probably going to be very uncomfortable. Her shortness of breath, frequent urination, heartburn, edema, and difficulty sleeping will only be getting worse. Fortunately, her shortness of breath may improve when the baby drops into her pelvis and puts less pressure on her lungs. Her cervix will start to thin out and open up, and her contractions will get stronger and more frequent. You will know that she has entered the first stage of labor when her contractions are regular, increasing in frequency, and lasting more than 30 seconds.

Breast Swelling

Mom's breasts will be filling with milk for the baby to drink when he is born. There may be some soreness from the stretching and leaking.

Constipation

Increased levels of the hormone progesterone during the last trimester will cause mom's digestive system to slow down. Pressure on her intestines by the uterus and her iron supplementation may be making it worse. If high-fiber foods and juice don't help, the doctor may prescribe a stool softener or a mild laxative.

Varicose Veins

Varicose veins are a result of the dilation of the blood vessels, usually caused by the extra blood formed during pregnancy and the increased pressure in the pelvis. They occur mostly in the legs and should cause only mild pain or discomfort.

Hemorrhoids

It is not uncommon for the blood vessels near the anus to dilate during late pregnancy and cause hemorrhoids. They can be itchy and painful, and they may bleed. If she can't get relief with over-the-counter products, she should let her doctor know.

What You Can Expect

You are probably getting pretty excited by now and really looking forward to having the baby finally arrive. You may also be a little anxious because of all the waiting and suspense from not knowing when the baby is actually going to arrive.

Feeling Peaceful and Happy

Having a baby may initially cause some stress because of all the new responsibilities and the uncertainty. You might also feel like it's going to limit your career or social options. However, if you accept that being a father is your most important job, you may find that you are feeling more peaceful. Having a strong sense of purpose can help keep you from being pulled in too many different directions at once. It will also make you happier.

Fear You Might Pass out at the Delivery

Every expectant father wonders if he has what it takes to get through the delivery without passing out. Some worry about the moment of birth, whereas for others the problem is blood and other bodily fluids. Believe it or not, except maybe on television, the fainting father is extremely uncommon. When somebody does pass out, it is because the emotion is so powerful that it leads to a type of response from the nervous system that slows down the heart and dilates the veins, thus dropping the blood pressure. If you are worried, the best thing you can do is make sure you are not dehydrated, you are reasonably well rested, and you have a purpose to serve during the birth. Idle spectators are more likely to be overwhelmed by emotion than a determined person with a job to do.

Fear That Your Relatives Are Going to Be Too Involved

You may have noticed your family hovering around more lately. Although the extra help may be welcome, you might be wondering if they are going to be around a bit too much. You have to remember that you and mom are not the only ones expecting. Your baby is going to be a new addition to both of your extended families as well. Suddenly your relatives have an instant reason to be intimately involved in your lives. After all, it is their grandchild, niece, or nephew. Depending on how excited your relatives are, this may or may not be a huge problem. Above all, as the parents you are ultimately in charge, and your relatives have to adhere to your wishes. Even the most overbearing mother- or father-in-law can be tamed if you and mom are united.

What's Going on with Prenatal Care

By now mom will be seeing the doctor at least once a week. The main reason for the visits is to assess if labor is imminent and to make sure that mom is prepared for the delivery. The doctor will be monitoring the baby's position and performing periodic vaginal examinations to assess mom's cervix. Although mom will likely be very anxious for the labor to start, her doctor will be hoping that it won't happen until at least week 37, so that the baby is full term.

Baby Position

Getting through the pelvis is a tight squeeze. To help, most babies get in a head-down position with their back toward the mother's front. This is called the face-down position, and it is the one most favored by doctors. About 5–10% of babies present with their back toward the mother's back. This is called the face-up position, and although it should not be a problem in the delivery, it is not as good as the face-down position. If the legs or buttocks are down instead, the baby is said to be breech.

Cervix Effacement

The cervix is normally a couple of centimeters thick. During labor, it will thin out and become shorter; this is called *effacement*. When the cervix is thick, it is said to be 0% effaced. When it is completely thinned out, it is said to be 100% effaced.

Cervix Dilation

For most of the pregnancy mom's cervix has been closed. However, it has to open up before the baby can come out. The cervix is usually dilated to around 4 centimeters when labor starts, and to 10 cm when it's time for the baby to come out. It is not uncommon for it to be 2–3 centimeters dilated for days, if not weeks, before labor starts. Once labor really gets going, the dilation can increase very rapidly.

If the baby is found to be breech and not moving on his own, the doctor will try to turn him by pressing and rubbing very hard on mom's abdomen. If her skin isn't hurting from the burning sensation, then the doctor isn't doing it hard enough. If that doesn't work, a cesarean section may be needed.

Baby Station

For the baby to come out, he needs to drop deep into the pelvis. How far the baby has descended into the pelvis is called the baby's *station*. The doctor or nurse will use certain parts of the pelvic bones as references and measure the distance, in centimeters, where the baby's head is relative to the pelvis. If the baby is fully engaged, he is said to be at zero station. If the baby has entered the pelvis but is not fully engaged, the station will be a negative number. For example, a -4 station means that the baby's head has 4 centimeters to go before being fully engaged. As the baby descends through the pelvis, the numbers will get progressively larger until the head crowns.

What You Two Should Be Discussing

It would be a good idea to review what you learned about labor and delivery from your readings or birthing classes. Also, if you two haven't decided whether the baby is going to be circumcised if he is a boy, you should decide now if you want the doctor to do it while in the hospital.

Three Stages of Labor

In order to understand what is happening during labor and delivery, and why, you need to understand the three stages of labor.

First Stage

The first stage is the longest part of the labor. It starts when the contractions become increasingly frequent (5–20 minutes apart) and longer lasting (about 30–45 seconds). The cervix is usually 100% effaced and roughly 3–4 centimeters dilated. The membranes may or may not have ruptured by this point. Toward the end of the first stage, the contractions have become very frequent (2–3 minutes apart) and are very intense (lasting about 60 seconds). When the cervix has dilated to 10 centimeters and the baby is engaged, it is time to push, and the first stage is complete.

Second Stage

The second stage of labor can be relatively short compared to the first stage. It starts when mom is 100% effaced, fully dilated, and ready to push. It ends when the baby is born, which is typically 30 minutes to 3 hours later. It may be sooner if this isn't her first baby.

Third Stage

The third stage of labor starts after the baby is born and is often referred to as the "afterbirth." This is the part where the placenta is delivered, and any lacerations or trauma are repaired, including the episiotomy, if one was done. Unless there are complications, it is very quick, typically lasting less than 15 minutes.

Circumcision

Circumcision involves surgically removing the foreskin of the penis. As you can imagine, anything that involves this area is going to be of great concern. However, recently there has been a lot of controversy surrounding circumcision. It is important to address this issue early, before the onset of labor, because you will be asked shortly after the birth whether you want it done or not. If you do, it can be done by the obstetrician as early as the second day of life.

Reasons for Circumcision

There are several reasons to circumcise your son. The most common are religious reasons (it is traditional for Jews and Muslims), conformity concerns (the majority of boys in the United States have undergone it), health reasons, and hygiene reasons.

Reasons Against Circumcision

There is a risk of complications when circumcision is performed, including bleeding, infection, and penile injury. There can also be a lot of pain, because many doctors don't use anesthesia. Ultimately you should also consider the fact that it may not be necessary, as the health benefits can be negated with good hygiene.

Contraception

Although mom won't be able to have sex for at least six weeks after the delivery, it is important to talk about contraception before things get too busy. It is a myth that you can't get pregnant after just giving birth and while breastfeeding. Although it may be true that mom is somewhat less fertile, many women report getting pregnant within a few months of giving birth.

What You Should Be Asking Yourself

Last month you were rushing around getting ready in case the baby came early. This month you will want to take care of any loose ends and make sure you are ready for what happens afterward.

Have I Finished up My Most Pressing Work?

Having a baby can be physically and emotionally demanding. During pregnancy it wasn't as much of an issue for you, but it definitely will be when the baby arrives. Babies spend a lot of time sleeping, but never for very long. Most have an inverted sleep schedule initially, sleeping mostly during the day and being up much of the night. This means that most parents of newborns do not get restful sleep and suffer from sleep deprivation to varying degrees. As a result, you should try to wrap up any really important or intensive projects and not start anything new or demanding around the time the baby is going to be born.

Am I Getting Enough Sleep and Relaxation?

Compounding the problem of sleep deprivation is the state of high anxiety and frustration new parents experience. There are going to be times in the middle of the night when the baby will be crying uncontrollably, and you and mom won't know what to do. To keep from getting too exhausted or frustrated, you should be getting as much sleep and relaxation as you can now. If you are already fatigued and stressed before the baby arrives, imagine what you will be like afterward.

Should I Make a Website or Blog?

Having a website or blog is a great way of communicating with family and friends. In addition to allowing you to communicate with a bunch of people at once, it also enables you to upload new pictures and video. It is even better if people are allowed to post their comments. If you are worried about security, you can use password protection to restrict it to family and friends.

What You Should Be Doing

Get the Digital Camera or Video Camera Ready

Some fathers want to videotape the labor and delivery and to take pictures of the baby to send to family and friends. If this is you, make sure that the batteries in both cameras are fully charged and you have an extra memory stick, videotape, or DVD disc.

Practice Driving the Route to the Hospital

Unless you are certain you won't get lost driving to the hospital in a hurry, especially at night, you should perform a test drive. Be sure you know where you are supposed to park. Leaving your car in front of the emergency room is rarely necessary or tolerated.

Preregister at the Hospital

Contact the labor and delivery floor at the hospital and see if you can register mom beforehand. It may help speed up the admission process and allow mom to avoid that painful wait when she finally goes into labor.

Make Sure You Are Prepared to Call People

In addition to making sure your cell phone is charged, you should write down all the names and telephone numbers of the people you are going to want to call when the baby is born. When the baby arrives, you may be too excited or tired to remember phone numbers that you would otherwise.

Get Her a Birth Gift

Mom has gone through a lot this last nine months and will be going through even more when the baby is born. It would be a thoughtful touch to buy her a gift for when the baby is born. It need not be jewelry or something expensive, but that wouldn't hurt either.

Appendix A: Potential Complications

Anemia—A state of having too few red blood cells. It can lead to significant symptoms, particularly fatigue. There are a number of causes, but iron deficiency is the most common. Inadequate body levels of iron before the pregnancy and/or not enough iron in the diet can lead to a deficiency later in the pregnancy. Fortunately, it is easily reversed with a change in diet and iron supplementation.

Arrested Labor—Occurs when the cervix stops dilating or the baby stops descending for more than two hours. Use of a medication called oxytocin may help, but if not, a cesarean section may be needed.

Blood Clots—Women are more susceptible to developing blood clots in the veins of their legs. If the vein is superficial and small, the condition is called *thrombophlebitis* and usually requires only rest, pain medications, leg elevation, and elastic stockings. If the vein is larger and deeper, the condition is called *deep vein thrombosis*

(DVT). DVT is potentially dangerous because a blood clot in one of these veins can break off and go to the lungs (causing a pulmonary embolus). A special type of ultrasound (Doppler) is required to make the diagnosis. Because of the serious risk posed by pulmonary emboli, treatment requires the extended use of blood thinners.

Breech Presentation—Near the end of the third trimester (weeks 32–36), most babies settle into a head-down position. When the baby presents with buttocks first instead of the head, it's called a breech presentation. Sometimes the baby rights himself before labor starts, or the doctor can turn the baby through a procedure called external cephalic version (ECV). If not, the baby may still be delivered vaginally, but it is a higher-risk procedure. In many cases, the safest (or the only) way to proceed is a cesarean section.

Chickenpox (Varicella)—Infection of the mother with this virus poses a serious risk to the baby. There are two periods of risk for the baby. The first is during the initial four months, when it can result in birth defects. The second is around the time the baby is born, when it can result in a severe infection. Since most women had chickenpox when they were younger, the chance of this happening is relatively low. However, if a woman is exposed and she hasn't had the disease or the vaccine, she should notify her doctor. She may end up needing varicella zoster immune globulin (VZIG).

Chorioamnionitis—An infection of the amniotic fluid and membranes surrounding the baby. It can be caused by a number of different organisms. There is a high risk of this type of infection when the membranes have been broken for more than 24 hours. However, infection can occur even if the membranes are intact and can actually lead to premature rupture of the membranes. Important signs in the mother are fever and an elevated white cell count in the blood.

Choriocarcinoma—An aggressive type of tumor seen following pregnancy, miscarriage, or abortion. It can grow quickly and spread widely. It is more common with molar pregnancies but can follow a normal pregnancy. It usually presents with continued bleeding. Despite its aggressiveness, it often responds well to chemotherapy.

Cleft Lip and Palate—Early on in development, there is a cleft or separation in the lip and palate. Normally the tissues that form the upper lip and palate come together and fuse. For some unclear reason, this does not happen in approximately 1 in 600 babies, and a birth defect results. This defect tends to be more common in Asians and boys. The condition is often first diagnosed by ultrasound, and surgery can usually repair it with few long-term consequences.

Colds and Flu—The chance of getting a cold or the flu during pregnancy is reasonably high. By themselves, these ailments are not particularly dangerous for the baby. The mother needs to make sure she takes in enough fluids to keep from being dehydrated. Fever medications such as acetaminophen and ibuprofen are generally safe (as are many cold and flu medications) when taken as directed and for a short time only.

Cord Prolapse—The condition where the umbilical cord falls into the birth canal before the baby. This can lead to the cord being compressed and the baby not getting enough blood or oxygen. It can lead to a slowdown of the baby's heart during contractions. Fortunately, it is relatively rare; but when it happens, it is a medical emergency and a cesarean section may be necessary.

Cystic Fibrosis (CF)—One of the most common genetic diseases in the United States. It has a devastating effect on the breathing and digestive functions. Most people with cystic fibrosis cannot survive beyond the second or third decade of life without a lung transplantation. Because CF requires two abnormal genes (one from each parent), either you or mom can be tested. If you have the gene but not the illness, you are a carrier. If both you and mom are carriers, then the odds are 1 in 4 that the baby is going to have the disease. Although it is more common in whites than in African Americans and Asian Americans, it is currently recommended that everyone get screened.

Cytomegalovirus (CMV)—CMV is a relatively common virus that most people are exposed to when they are younger. There is a risk (albeit small) of birth defects if the mother develops a CMV during pregnancy. Because a large number of preschoolers carry the virus, there is sometimes concern about whether a pregnant woman should avoid young children during pregnancy. If the mother has antibodies against CMV, she is likely protected. If she doesn't, the baby could be at risk, but the odds of something bad happening are low.

Down's Syndrome—One of the most common chromosomal disorders. It results from an extra copy of chromosome 21, and it causes mental retardation and other birth defects. The older the mother, the more likely it is to occur. Diagnosing it requires taking cells from either the amniotic fluid (amniocentesis) or the placenta (chorionic villus sampling) and looking at the structure of the chromosomes. Screening for Down's syndrome using blood tests is performed in practically every pregnancy.

Early Miscarriage—When the pregnancy spontaneously ends before week 12. It is relatively common, occurring in 10–15% of pregnancies, with the highest risk during the first trimester. It is often nature's way of stopping a pregnancy when the genetic or chromosomal circumstances are just not right (abnormal fetus).

Eclampsia—A severe form of pregnancy-induced high blood pressure that can occur if preeclampsia is untreated and allowed to progress. In addition to high blood pressure and protein in the urine, eclampsia is accompanied by severe headache, nausea or vomiting, convulsions, and/or coma. Treatment involves immediate termination of the pregnancy as well as controlling the blood pressure and seizures. Fortunately, it is very rare with good prenatal care.

Ectopic Pregnancy—Normally the egg is fertilized in the Fallopian tube and travels to the uterus. Sometimes the egg fails to leave the Fallopian tube. When this happens, it is called a tubal, or ectopic, pregnancy, and a normal pregnancy is not possible. Over time, the fetus grows, and if pregnancy is not terminated, it will lead to a rupture in the Fallopian tube with catastrophic results. Therefore, an ectopic pregnancy is a life-threatening condition normally corrected with an abortion.

Fetal Alcohol Syndrome—An array of birth defects involving mental retardation; abnormalities of the face, limbs, and heart; as well as growth problems. It is caused by exposure to excessive alcohol, particularly during the first trimester, when the baby's organs are developing. It is one of the few birth defects that is 100% preventable.

Fetal Distress—A situation where the baby is thought to be in distress, usually discovered by monitoring the baby's heart rate. For example, sudden slowing during a contraction implies that the baby is not getting enough blood and oxygen. Because of the serious risk, the treatment is immediate delivery of the baby.

Fever—There is some concern that the mother's having a high fever (>102°F) can lead to birth defects (especially during the first trimester). In most cases, acetaminophen or ibuprofen is effective in reducing the temperature.

Fifth Disease—A childhood disease that causes fever and a characteristic rash. Although many women have had the disease by the time they are adults, they may not have realized it, because the symptoms can be mild or it was not diagnosed. Because infection with the virus (parvovirus B19) that causes the disease has been known to cause miscarriages and a severe form of anemia, some women are concerned about being near small children during pregnancy. Although it is a concern, the risk is probably not that high.

Gestational Diabetes—A temporary type of diabetes that occurs during pregnancy. It results when the mother's pancreas is not able to make enough insulin to keep her glucose levels normal. Its presence may be suspected based on the detection of sugar spilling into the urine using a urine dipstick. Elevated blood levels can confirm the diagnosis. The treatment is good control of blood sugar during pregnancy. Poor control of blood sugar can place both the mother and the baby at risk.

Group B Streptococcus (GBS)—Newborns infected with the bacteria group B streptococcus can become extremely ill and die shortly after birth. Since GBS can be found in the birth canal of many women, babies born after a prolonged membrane rupture can be at risk. Most women undergo a swab of their cervix before labor starts (after week 35) to test for the bacteria. If it is present, antibiotics will be given at the time of labor. The bacteria easily succumb to the treatment.

HELLP Syndrome—A severe complication of preeclampsia or eclampsia. HELLP syndrome usually presents with elevated blood pressure, headache, progressive nausea and vomiting, and upper abdominal pain. It can lead to severe liver damage and bleeding. To protect the life of the mother (as well as the baby), the pregnancy is induced or cesarean section is performed as soon as possible.

Hepatitis B (HBV)—HBV is a virus that can cause both acute and chronic inflammation of the liver. HBV poses a risk for the baby at the time of birth when there is contact with the mother's infected blood. By knowing in advance if this is an issue, it is possible to protect the baby with special antibodies (immune globulin) and vaccines.

Human Immunodeficiency Virus (HIV)—HIV poses a risk for the baby at the time of birth when there is contact with the mother's infected blood. Use of antiviral medications during pregnancy can reduce the risk of transmitting the virus. As a result, more and more states are requiring that it be screened for during a prenatal workup.

Hyperemesis Gravidarum—A severe form of nausea and vomiting that affects most pregnant women. It can be so bad that it leads to fluid and electrolyte disorders, weight loss, and nutritional deficiencies. It may require admission to the hospital for intravenous nutrition and anti-nausea medications. It tends to resolve by week 20.

Incompetent Cervix—A cervix that is too weak to withstand the pressure placed on it by the growing baby. It is rare (1% of pregnancies), but it can cause miscarriage or premature delivery. It usually occurs during the second trimester and can be treated by sewing the cervix closed (called a cerclage). The suture is removed after week 36 in preparation for the birth.

Intrauterine-Growth Restriction (IUGR)—A term referring to a baby that is growing at a slower rate than normal (<10th percentile). It is based on ultrasound findings involving the baby's head, abdomen, and legs. The most common cause is a problem with the placenta. It can also be caused by too little amniotic fluid, certain birth defects or genetic disorders, and diseases involving the mother. The baby will need to be monitored more closely, will likely be born small, and may have to stay in the hospital a little longer before going home.

Late Miscarriage—The spontaneous termination of pregnancy during the second trimester up to week 20. Unlike an early miscarriage, it has less to do with chromosomal abnormalities and more to do with conditions affecting the uterus, placenta, and cervix, as well as issues related to the mother's health (such as diabetes or high blood pressure) or to infections.

Measles—A relatively rare viral infection that may cause an increased risk of miscarriage. Most women were vaccinated for measles when they were children, and therefore are immune. Women who weren't vaccinated should not get the vaccine until their pregnancy is over.

Meconium Staining—The baby's first bowel movement is called meconium, and it usually occurs after the baby is born. If the baby passes the meconium before labor, it can make the amniotic fluid dark. It can be a sign of fetal stress and may occasionally cause issues with the baby's breathing. Most babies with meconium staining do very well, especially if they are past their due date.

Molar Pregnancy—A type of tumor that is also called a hydatidiform mole. A normal conception takes place, but it does not result in a viable pregnancy. The placenta is abnormal and on ultrasound is often described as looking like a bag of grapes. If a fetus develops, it is very abnormal.

Mumps—A relatively rare viral infection that can cause miscarriage and preterm labor. It is not very common because most mothers have been vaccinated against it. Exposure to someone with the mumps should be reported to the doctor, but it is unlikely that the disease will develop.

Overdue Pregnancy—A baby is considered overdue or post-term if the pregnancy is at week 42 or later. Many "post-term babies" may not actually be overdue; it is not uncommon for women to get the date of their last menstrual period wrong. If the baby appears too well developed, most doctors will induce labor.

Placenta Abruption—An abrupt separation of the placenta from the uterus, also called *abruptio placenta*. It is a common cause of bleeding late in pregnancy. The blood loss ranges from light to heavy, and there can be abdominal pain from strong uterine contractions. Although ultrasound is helpful in diagnosis, it can't definitely rule it out. When the separation is small, treatment includes bed rest for a couple of days. With larger separations, blood transfusions and other emergency treatment may be necessary. The prognosis is good with close medical monitoring.

Placenta Accreta—A condition where the placenta grows too deep into the uterus and becomes stuck. It tends to happen when there is scarring from previous surgeries or deliveries. After childbirth, the placenta isn't able to detach, and there is excessive bleeding. Treatment usually requires removing the placenta surgically. At times, it may be necessary to remove the uterus as well to stop the bleeding.

Placenta Previa—An abnormally low placement of the placenta. This occurs when the placenta is attached to the lower part of the uterus, particularly near the cervix. It usually presents with painless, bright red bleeding, particularly in the third trimester. Diagnosis is usually made by ultrasound. Mild bleeding is usually treated conservatively with bed rest; more severe bleeding may require hospitalization for close monitoring. The goal is to continue the pregnancy for as long as possible. Most women require a cesarean section, especially if the placenta is too close to the cervix.

Postpartum Bleeding—Refers to heavy bleeding (or hemorrhaging) after delivery. Fortunately, it is rare, but when it happens, it can be severe and life threatening. Although it usually occurs immediately after childbirth, it can be delayed up to a couple of weeks if it is due to retained pieces of the placenta. Common causes include a uterus that doesn't fully contract or cuts (lacerations) involving the uterus, cervix, or vagina.

Preeclampsia—A form of pregnancy-related high blood pressure. Although the exact cause isn't known, it is known that certain toxic substances are produced. In addition to a rise in blood pressure, there is protein in the urine (detected by urine dipstick). In more severe cases, there can be swelling of the hands and face as well as an abrupt weight gain. Untreated preeclampsia can progress to a severe form called eclampsia. The definitive treatment is induction of labor or cesarean section.

Premature Labor—Refers to labor that starts after week 20 (when the baby is likely to survive) and before week 37 (considered full term). There are numerous potential causes. If the membranes are intact and the cervix is closed, it is often possible to suppress labor (usually through medications) until the baby is more mature. Bed rest and avoidance of sexual intercourse are important. Hospitalization for closer monitoring may be required.

Premature Rupture of the Membranes (PROM)—This occurs when the chorionic membranes rupture ("water breaks") before labor starts (contractions). Sometimes it's obvious, with a gushing of fluid, and other times it can be a slow leak. With the latter, the doctor can test some of the fluid to be sure. It usually requires the mother to be hospitalized for monitoring and assessment for infection. If the baby is mature enough, labor is usually induced.

Rh Incompatibility—A condition where the mother produces antibodies against the baby's red blood cells. It occurs when the father has red blood cells with the Rh factor (type of red cell marker), and the mother does not. If the mother was exposed to Rh factor during a previous pregnancy, she likely developed antibodies against it. These antibodies can cross the placenta and attack the blood cells of the baby. If severe, it can lead to blood transfusions for the baby or even loss of the pregnancy. Today there are Rh vaccines available to keep the mother from developing Rh antibodies.

Rubella—Exposure to rubella (German measles) during the first trimester can lead to serious birth defects. The risk is greatest during the first month and decreases over time. After the third month (when the organs are in place), the risk significantly drops. Most women are immune to rubella, either because they had the illness before or because they received the vaccine. The doctor usually checks for immunity early in prenatal care.

Sickle Cell Anemia—A genetic disorder that results in an abnormal form of hemoglobin. It leads to abnormally shaped red blood cells, blocking of small blood vessels, and severe anemia. Approximately 1 in 12 African Americans is a carrier (has the gene but not the disease). If both parents are carriers, the baby has a 1 in 4 chance of getting the disease. Although it mainly affects African Americans, it can affect people of Mediterranean and Middle Eastern descent.

Shoulder Dystocia—Refers to the baby's shoulder getting stuck in the birth canal. This is a serious condition because the baby's head has already come out.

Spina Bifida—A birth defect where there is an opening of the spine. Early in the pregnancy, the baby's nervous system starts as a sheet of cells and rolls into a tube. Spina bifida results if the tube that is to become the spinal cord doesn't form properly. Although surgery can repair this defect, significant damage to the spinal cord and nerves can remain. Taking folic acid before and during the pregnancy can help, but not totally prevent, this defect.

Stillbirth—Refers to the birth of baby that has died after week 20 and usually before the start of labor. The first clue is when the baby stops moving around and kicking. An ultrasound can confirm the loss. In many cases, it is totally unexpected because the pregnancy is without complications. The baby is not usually expelled, and labor must be induced. Afterward, the baby, placenta, and umbilical cord are examined to determine what went wrong. Unfortunately, the answer isn't always discovered.

Tay-Sachs Disease—A genetic disorder that results in an enzyme disorder leading to the buildup of a toxic substance in the nerve cells and tissues in the brain. Although Tay-Sachs babies start out life normally, they become severely disabled and usually die before their fifth birthday. It is prominent among the Jewish population of Eastern European descent, French Canadians, and Louisiana Cajuns, but it can be found in other ethnic groups as well.

Thalassemia—A genetic disorder involving an abnormal form of hemoglobin. However, unlike sickle cell anemia, the red cells produced do not clog the blood vessels. Instead, there is an underproduction of normal hemoglobin, leading to mild to moderately severe anemia. In very severe cases (called hydrops fetalis), the baby usually dies soon after birth. The abnormal gene is more common in people of Italian, Greek, and other Mediterranean ancestry.

Threatened Miscarriage—This occurs when there is bleeding and the possibility of a miscarriage during the first 16 weeks, requiring close monitoring of the baby. If mom is examined and the cervix is open, miscarriage is considered inevitable. Complete bed rest is sometimes recommended, but it may not help. At the very least, sex and strenuous activity should be avoided until the bleeding stops.

Toxoplasmosis—Birth defects from toxoplasmosis are very rare, but when they happen, they can be very serious. Although antibiotics are available, it is difficult to know if the mother or the baby has been infected. It is usually recommended that pregnant women avoid cats to prevent the illness in the first place. Avoiding stool or the cat box is particularly important.

Urinary Tract Infection (UTI)—UTIs are very common during pregnancy. There is a significant risk that a bladder infection (the most common type of UTI) can lead to a severe kidney infection. If this happens, there is an increased risk of miscarriage. Most doctors screen for bacteria in the blood during the first prenatal visit and periodically with a urine dipstick. UTIs are relatively easy to treat with antibiotics. However, sometimes it is necessary to be admitted to the hospital for intravenous antibiotics and fluids.

Uterine Inversion—Very rarely the placenta does not detach from the uterus as it should and as a result is pulled inside out. This can lead to significant bleeding and requires the uterus to be cleaned out and placed back in.

Uterine Rupture—Very rarely the uterus tears or ruptures during labor. It usually happens because of a scar from a previous cesarean section or uterus surgery. When it happens, it usually presents as severe bleeding and requires surgical repair. Sometimes the damage is too extensive, and the uterus needs to be removed. In cases where there is risk of uterine rupture, the doctor may recommend avoiding a vaginal delivery and going straight to an elective cesarean section.

Appendix B: Glossary

Active Labor—When the cervix is dilated between 4 and 8 cm, and the contractions are about 3–5 minutes apart.

Afterbirth—The placenta and amniotic membranes that are discharged after the baby is delivered.

Alpha-fetoprotein (AFP)—A substance produced by the baby but found in the mother's blood and the amniotic fluid. It is used to screen for birth defects.

Amniocentesis—A procedure involving removing fluid from the amniotic sac with a needle. It is used to test for various diseases, including Down's syndrome.

Amniotic Fluid—The fluid inside the amniotic sac and surrounding the baby.

Amniotic Sac—A membrane that surrounds and contains the baby, placenta, and the amniotic fluid.

APGAR Score—A measurement of the baby's well-being, taken 1 minute and 5 minutes after birth.

Areola—The colored area surrounding the nipple.

Augmented Labor—Stalled labor that is treated with a contraction stimulant called oxytocin or by the trade name Pitocin®.

Back Labor—Labor pain that is felt in the back instead of the abdomen.

Bilirubin—A by-product of red blood cell destruction that is removed by the liver.

Biophysical Profile—A comprehensive baby well-being test sometimes performed in the third trimester.

Birthing Center—A medical facility specializing in the delivery of babies. It may be part of a hospital or a separate freestanding entity.

Bishop Score—A measurement of the likelihood of success when inducing labor.

Blood Pressure Check—Checking for changes in blood pressure is used to monitor for potential complications in the pregnancy.

Blood Sugar Test—See Glucose Tolerance Test.

Blood Typing—A method for determining what blood type the mother is.

Bloody Show—A bloody vaginal discharge late in pregnancy that often precedes labor.

Braxton-Hicks Contractions—Irregular and painless contractions of the uterus during the third trimester. These are not labor contractions.

Canavan Disease Screening—Blood test used to screen for Canavan disease in those of Ashkenazi Jewish decent.

Cervical Cultures—Testing of the cervix for sexually transmitted diseases. It is usually performed after a PAP smear.

Cervix—The opening of the uterus or womb.

Cesarean Section—Surgical delivery of the baby through the abdomen.

Chorionic Villus Sampling (CVS)—A biopsy of the area between the uterus and what will become the placenta. It is used to test for genetic defects earlier than an amniocentesis.

Chromosomal Abnormality—An abnormal number or structure of a chromosome, leading to birth defects.

Chromosome—A distinct grouping of genes. Humans normally have 23 pairs, or 46 chromosomes.

Colostrum—The first milk that comes from a mother's breast. It is thinner and more watery than the milk produced later during nursing.

Complete Blood Count—A blood test used to measure the red blood cell count and to look for infections.

Congenital—Present from birth. *Congenital defect* is often used interchangeably with *birth defect*.

Contraction—A tightening of the uterus.

Contraction Stress Test—A measurement of the baby's response to uterine contractions. It is sometimes used as a baby well-being test during the third trimester.

Crown-to-Rump Length—The length from the top of the head (crown) to the buttocks (rump). It is used when the baby is curled up and the legs are no longer stretched out.

Dilation—Refers to how open the cervix is. It typically ranges from 0–10 centimeters.

Doppler—A type of ultrasound device that allows one to hear the baby's heartbeat.

Down's Syndrome—A chromosomal abnormality involving an extra chromosome 21 (three instead of two). It is one of the most common birth defects.

Due Date—The date that the baby is expected to be born, plus or minus two weeks. It is usually based on the mother's last menstrual period.

Early Labor—The first part of labor, when the contractions become regular, frequent, and prolonged. This is usually the time to start getting to the hospital or birthing center.

Effacement—Refers to how thinned out the cervix is. It ranges from 0% (no thinning) to 100% (completely thinned out).

Embryo—Refers to the baby during the first 10 weeks of gestation.

Endometrium—The inside lining of the uterus where the fertilized egg is initially inserted.

Enema—Cleaning out of the bowel by introducing fluid into the rectum.

Epidural Block—Injection of an anesthetic around the spinal cord. It is one of the most common forms of pain control during labor.

Episiotomy—Surgical cutting of the area behind the vagina and above the rectum (called the perineum). It is used to help prevent large tears as the baby's head passes through the birth canal.

External Cephalic Version (ECV)—A procedure used to rotate a baby that is breeched. It is often performed in an attempt to avoid a cesarean section.

Fallopian Tube—The tube connecting the ovary to the uterus. The woman's egg is usually fertilized here.

False Labor—Contractions or tightening of the uterus without leading to dilation of the cervix.

Fasting Blood Sugar—A blood test measuring the blood glucose level after fasting overnight. An elevated level may indicate gestational diabetes.

Fertilization—The joining of a man's sperm with a woman's egg.

Fetal Distress—Indications that something is wrong with the baby. It usually results in an immediate delivery of the baby.

Fetal Fibronectin (fFN) Test —A test performed to see if there is an increased risk for a premature delivery. The test is positive if fFN is found in the secretions of the birth canal.

Fetal Monitor—A device used to monitor the baby's heartbeat. Monitoring is usually done externally by placing a probe on the mother's abdomen.

Fetus—Refers to the baby from the tenth week of gestation until the baby is born.

Forceps—A tong-like instrument sometimes placed around the baby's head to help guide the baby through and out of the birth canal. It can cause serious damage if not used by a skilled physician.

Full Term—Refers to a baby that is born after week 38.

Gestational Age—The age of the baby, in weeks, starting with the first day of the last menstrual period. Fertilization or conception occurs the third week of gestation.

Glucose Tolerance Test (GTT)—A blood test used to screen for gestational diabetes by assessing the mother's response to a sugar load. The test is considered positive if her blood sugar level is elevated in response to drinking a sugary solution.

Glucosuria—Glucose or sugar in the urine. Usually indicates diabetes that is not well controlled.

Group B Streptococcus (GBS) Test—A test for the GBS bacteria in or near the mother's birth canal. If present, treatment with antibiotics is usually necessary during labor to protect the baby.

Hematocrit—The percentage of the plasma or blood volume made up of red blood cells. It is important in diagnosing anemia.

Hemoglobin—The part of the red blood cell that binds oxygen. Measuring its levels can also be used to screen for anemia.

Hepatitis B Antibodies Test—Blood tests used to assess if the mother has been exposed to or has the hepatitis B virus. Treatment at the time of birth is important to prevent the baby from getting infected.

High-Risk Pregnancy—A pregnancy involving complications that place the mother and baby at higher risk. Requires the care of a specially trained physician or perinatologist.

Home Uterine Monitoring—A test that involves the recording of the woman's contractions at home and transmitting the data to the doctor by telephone. It is sometimes used for women at risk of premature labor.

Human Chorionic Gonadotropin (HCG)—A hormone produced early in pregnancy and used to confirm pregnancy as well as screen for birth defects.

Hydramnios—An increased amount of amniotic fluid.

Hydrocephalus—An excessive amount of fluid surrounding the brain.

Hypertension—High blood pressure.

Hypotension—Low blood pressure.

In Utero—Inside or within the uterus.

Induced Labor—Labor that is started or induced through the use of medications or a procedure. It is often used with a post term baby or prolonged rupture of membranes.

Insulin—A hormone produced by the pancreas that helps the body utilize glucose. Synthetic insulin is used to treat diabetes.

In Utero Insider—or within the uterus.

Isoimmunization—Development of antibodies against certain types of red blood cells. It often occurs when an Rh-negative woman has an Rh-positive baby or receives an Rh-positive blood transfusion.

Jaundice—An excessive amount of bilirubin in the blood. It is relatively common in newborns and may require treatment (phototherapy) to prevent brain damage.

Kick Count—A measurement of how often the baby moves or kicks over a certain time period. It may be used to assess a baby's well-being during the third trimester.

Labor—The process where contractions of the uterus lead to dilation and effacement of the cervix and ejection of the baby.

Lightening—Changes in the uterus leading to the baby "dropping" into the pelvis. It often occurs several weeks before labor starts.

Lochia—The vaginal discharge that occurs the first few weeks after the birth.

Meconium—The baby's first bowel movement. It is usually greenish-yellow and thick, and occurs shortly after birth.

Miscarriage—The premature termination of a pregnancy before week 20.

Morning Sickness—The nausea and vomiting associated with early pregnancy. It is thought to be caused by the surge in pregnancy hormones.

Mutations—Abnormalities or changes to genes.

Neural Tube Defects—Abnormalities involving the development of the brain and spinal cord.

Nuchal Translucency Screening—A special ultrasound test used in conjunction with blood testing to screen for Down's syndrome.

Nurse-Midwife—A nurse with additional training and certification in pregnancy and the delivery of babies.

Obstetrician—A physician with specialized training in the care of pregnant women and the delivery of babies.

Oligohydramnios—An abnormally small amount of amniotic fluid.

Ovulation—The periodic or cyclic release of a woman's egg from her ovaries. Fertilization or conception most usually occurs within a couple days of ovulation.

Oxytocin—A synthetic version of the natural hormone that causes contractions of the uterus. It is often called by its brand name, Pitocin®, and used to induce or augment labor.

Pap Smear—A test used to screen for cancer or precancerous lesions of the cervix.

Pediatrician—A physician specializing in the care of babies and children.

Pelvic Exam—A physical examination of the birth canal, cervix, and uterus. It is performed at the end of the pregnancy to assess the progress of labor.

Percutaneous Umbilical Blood Sampling (PUBS)—An invasive test that involves taking blood from the umbilical cord with a needle. It is used primarily to test for chromosome abnormalities, blood disorders, and infections of the baby.

Perinatologist—A physician specially trained in high-risk pregnancies.

Perineum—The area between the genitals and the rectum. It is an area prone to tearing during delivery.

Phosphatidyl Glycerol (PG)—A substance made when the baby's lungs are mature. It is measured when deciding if the baby is mature enough to be delivered early.

Phototherapy—Light therapy used to treat neonatal jaundice or high levels of bilirubin in the baby.

Placenta—An organ that connects the baby's umbilical cord to the mother's uterus. It is critical for growth and development.

Postdate Birth—A birth occurring during or after week 42 of gestation.

Postpartum—The six-week period after the baby is born.

Premature Birth—A birth occurring before week 38 of gestation.

Presentation—Refers to how the baby is entering the birth canal or which body part is coming first.

Proteinuria—Protein in the urine. Found with urinary tract infections, preeclampsia, and kidney disease.

Pudendal Block—A type of local anesthesia administered as a shot during labor.

Pyelonephritis—Urinary tract infection involving the kidneys. A serious infection in a pregnant woman.

Quad-Screen Test—A screening test for birth defects. It consists of four blood tests, including alpha-fetoprotein, human chorionic gonadotropin, unconjugated estriol, and inhibin-A.

Quickening—Feeling the baby kicking or moving.

Rh-Factor—A red blood cell marker found in about 85% of people.

Rh-Negative—A person who does not have the Rh-factor. See Isoimmunization.

RhoGAM—A medication given to an Rh-negative mother during and after pregnancy to prevent antibodies to the Rh-factor.

Rubella Titers—A blood test checking for antibodies or immunity against rubella or the German measles.

Rupture of Membranes—The breaking of the amniotic sac. It usually leads to a sudden loss of amniotic fluid or "water breaking." Sometimes it is a slow leak.

Silent Labor—Dilation of the cervix without the pain from contractions.

Sonogram—See Ultrasound.

Spinal Block—Injection of an anesthetic into the spinal cord. It is not used as much as the epidural block during labor. It is, however, often used during a cesarean section.

Station—An estimate of where the baby is in the birth canal. The higher the positive number, the farther along the baby is.

Trimester—A method of tracking pregnancy using three equal periods of about 3 months or 13 weeks each.

Triple-Screen Test—A screening test for birth defects. It consists of three blood tests, including alpha-fetoprotein, human chorionic gonadotropin, and unconjugated estriol.

Ultrasound—A noninvasive and safe test used to examine the baby inside the womb. It involves bouncing sounds waves off the baby.

Umbilical Cord—The cord connecting the baby to the mother. It is the baby's lifeline to the placenta.

Urinalysis—A test used to screen for urinary tract infections, gestational diabetes, and preeclampsia.

Urine Culture—A test used to identify the bacteria causing a urinary tract infection.

Uterus—The female organ where a baby grows and develops. A woman's womb.

Vacuum Extractor—A suctioning instrument sometimes placed on top of the baby's head to help guide the baby through and out of the birth canal.

Vagina—The birth canal.

Vena Cava—The major vein that returns blood from the body to the heart. Compression of it by the uterus can lead to low blood pressure.

Appendix C: World Wide Web Resources

Websites

About.com
http://fatherhood.about.com

Ask Dr. Sears
http://www.askdrsears.com

Baby Center
http://www.babycenter.com

Breastfeeding Basics
http://www.breastfeedingbasics.com

Dr. Spock.com
http://www.DrSpock.com

Edads.com
http://edads.com

Entrepreneurial Parent
http://www.en-parent.com

EverythingForParents.com
http://www.everythingforparents.com

Family.com
http://family.go.com

Green Home
http://www.greenhome.com

MrDad.com
http://www.mrdad.com

Pregnancy Today
http://www.pregnancytoday.com

U.S. Savings Bonds
http://www.savingsbonds.gov

Vaccine Education Center
http://www.vaccine.chop.edu

Organizations

American Academy of Pediatrics
http://www.aap.org

American Academy of Family Physicians
http://www.aafp.com

American Association of Birth Centers
http://www.birthcenters.org

American College of Nurse-Midwives
http://www.midwife.org

American College of Obstetricians and Gynecologists
http://www.acog.com

American Council of Life Insurers
http://www.acli.com

Au Pair Search
http://www.aupairsearch.com

College Savings Plans Network
http://www.collegesavings.org

Debtors Anonymous
http://www.debtorsanonymous.com

Doulas of North America
http://www.dona.com

Families and Work Institute
http://www.familiesandwork.org

Financial Planning Association
http://www.fpanet.org

Insurance Information Institute
http://www.iii.org

International Nanny Association
http://www.nanny.org

March of Dimes
http://www.modimes.org

National Foundation for Credit Counseling
http://www.nfcc.org

National Safety Council
http://www.nsc.org

Spina Bifida Association
http://www.sbaa.org

The Father's Network
http://www.fathersnetwork.org

U.S. Consumer Product Safety Commission
http://www.cpsc.gov

Index

B

C

D

H

M

N

O

P

Q

Quality time, 192, 212

R

Radiation, 48, 54
Records. *See* Documenting baby
Recovery from birth, 16–17
Red blood cells, 57–58
Relationship changes, 221, 222. *See also* Communication
Relatives
    birth team, on, 70–71
    genetic disorders of, 56
    loans from, 109
    proximity to, 82
    relationships with, 222, 227–228
    support from, 122
Residents (medical), 71
Responsibilities of father. *See* Father, role of
Restaurant costs, 104
Reticence, 170–171
Retirement, 107, 114, 137–140
Rh compatibility, 58, 63, 167, 210
Ripening the cervix, 76
Rubella (German measles), 60, 167

S

Saddle black, 75
Safety, 36–37, 44–48, 81, 84, 85, 87–89, 166
Salmonella, 37
Satisfaction. *See* Happiness, achieving
Saunas, 46
Savings, 107–108, 180. *See also* Finances
Scarring, mother's, 53
Schools, 82

About the Author

Brian Lipps, M.D., is the proud father of three young boys and knows firsthand the types of problems that expecting and new fathers face, particularly those related to feeding, sleeping, and the health of the baby. His medical training has been particularly valuable when dealing with health, safety, and developmental issues including common illnesses and recognizing important cognitive, motor, emotional, language, and personality milestones. Dr. Lipps lives in Norfolk, VA.